IF JEWELS
COULD TALK

IF JEWELS COULD TALK

Seven secret histories

CAROL WOOLTON

GALLERY BOOKS UK

First published in Great Britain by Gallery Books, an imprint of
Simon & Schuster UK Ltd, 2024

1 3 5 7 9 10 8 6 4 2

Simon & Schuster UK Ltd
1st Floor
222 Gray's Inn Road
London WC1X 8HB

www.simonandschuster.co.uk
www.simonandschuster.com.au
www.simonandschuster.co.in

Simon & Schuster Australia, Sydney
Simon & Schuster India, New Delhi

A CIP catalogue record for this book is available from the British Library

Hardback ISBN: 978-1-3985-2693-8
Trade Paperback ISBN: 978-1-3985-2694-5
eBook ISBN: 978-1-3985-2695-2

Typeset in Sabon by M Rules
Printed and Bound in the UK using 100% Renewable Electricity
at CPI Group (UK) Ltd

MIX
Paper | Supporting
responsible forestry
FSC
www.fsc.org
FSC® C171272

To Stella, Agnes, Marina, Coco, Ivy, Celine and Jean –
in anticipation of future jewellery enthusiasts.

CONTENTS

INTRODUCTION

As I walk down any given street, I'm always struck by the fact that everyone I pass by is wearing an item of jewellery in some form. Be it a battered wedding ring, a woven wrist band or a small silver hoop in their ear, jewellery really is everywhere we look. As jewellery editor of *British Vogue* for decades and an author who's written widely on the subject, I have often reflected on why this is, and when looking back over the history of jewellery, I can only conclude that it fulfils a primal urge to decorate ourselves.

Indeed, early humans were engaging in self-adornment long before they daubed ochre paintings on cave walls, making it one of humanity's longest-running cultural traditions. Our ancestors used anything they could get their hands on – teeth, talons, feathers, shells, pebbles – to string together primitive necklaces, chokers, bracelets and head ornaments and, although humble, these acted as hugely sophisticated communicators, not only functioning as protective amulets for safety and well-being, but also as tribal signifiers. Jewellery then, as now, could set the wearer apart and yet simultaneously provide a vital link to the tribe to which a person belonged.

Clothes were worn for practicality, warmth and modesty, whereas body decoration told a far more subjective and personal tale of the wearer's status within their community. From a tooth or claw pendant we could learn of an individual's prowess as a hunter, whilst other jewels might speak of beloved family members or a god that was worshipped. Whilst excavating Viking graves, for example, archaeologists have found many pendants in the shape of a hammer, evidence of the cult surrounding Thor, the Norse god of thunder and storms, who wielded his Mjolnir hammer to deal deadly blows to his enemy. Similarly, we can tell who was Christian by the relics they wore and left behind. The most common design for cameo rings discovered in Britain from the Roman era feature the snake-haired Medusa, suggesting she was used as an apotropaic symbol to ward off evil, much like the modern-day belief in the protective powers of the 'evil eye'. A sacred turtle was worn in China to communicate hope for a long life.

Whatever its form, jewellery invariably spoke to the lifeblood and spirit of a person, and its ability to express the essence of an individual without having to say a word continues to this day. Modern jewellery, just as that of our ancestors, functions as an outward sign of our core beliefs, our ethnicity, kinfolk, astrological signs, our homes and family. Within these small structures has always been found the loves, sorrows and philosophy of human existence. If you ever find yourself stuck for conversation, ask the other person about the jewellery they are wearing, as there will inevitably be a story. A chance comment I made at a party about a ring worn by *Game of Thrones* actress Laura Pradelska led to a long and emotional conversation about her Jewish family history during the Holocaust. Many of her family perished, but the stone in the ring survived to tell the tale of suffering, bravery and love. Nothing we wear defines us in quite the same way as jewellery and yet it links us all to a collective consciousness, one which is not divided by borders, religion, gender or language. Whilst specific signs and codes might vary from generation to generation, the essence of jewellery remains the same. It shines bright as an art form in all our lives as a way to identify, both ourselves and others, and communicate. Through our jewellery choices we can be noticed, seen and heard. You could call it the unique global connector, linking human beings across the world today as well as to our ancestors lost in the mists of time.

Every civilization has divulged its secrets through surviving ornaments, and from the beginning, precious stones and metal have been used as a ritual of style as well as a form of portable currency. We might wear jewellery as a symbolic glittering identity tag – items like wedding rings, tiaras and charm bracelets all have the capacity to express a small part of who we are and how we live now – or simply to add a splash of colour and sparkle to an outfit. As a jewellery editor for thirty years, I've written countless features for *Vogue* and *Tatler* about current trends whilst draping dazzlingly extravagant gems on supermodels. Yes, jewels can signal a certain type of lavishness and wealth, but even though the jewels I'm arranging for a photoshoot might be the latest diamond-encrusted collection, there's also something deeply primal about the repetition of jewels worn in the same places on a body to deliver a message. It was ever thus.

I'm fascinated by the cyclical nature of jewellery and the fundamental basics that never alter. The world around us may change beyond recognition, but the motifs and symbolism in jewellery remain the same. If I walked out of London's V&A Museum tomorrow wearing the Shannongrove gorget neckpiece, which looks as fresh as the day it was created, I know I'd be asked where I bought it or the name of the new designer who created it. That wouldn't be possible with fashion or technology from the past, nor anything else that we use today.

Sometimes it's more than the materials or decoration of a jewel that tells the story of the era. Recently, an exceptionally preserved deer tooth pendant from the Upper Palaeolithic period was unearthed in a Siberian cave, and from the DNA extracted from human skin cells and sweat molecules found on the piece, historians identified the wearer as a female of North Eurasian ancestry who lived 19,000–25,000 years ago. Most likely the pendant was a prized gift from one of the hunters in her group, a symbol of their prowess and ability to provide food, allowing archaeologists to build a picture of how society was run as well as the social connections that would have surrounded her at the time. Researchers believe that notches made in eagle claws found amongst Neanderthal remains in Croatia indicate that these claws were mounted into a bracelet or necklace 130,000 years ago, before *Homo sapiens* arrived in Europe. This goes to show that all species appreciated jewellery and, gradually, we can learn more about their lives from these artefacts.

As well as items of personal significance, humans have always clung to certain cherished motifs and designs for their jewellery, and they act as signifiers of how humans have lived and evolved through history. The first metallic shape used to attach two pieces of material together and the grandiose 152.35-carat sapphire panther pin worn by the Duchess of Windsor are both brooches, after all, and each one just as effectively expresses who the wearer was and how they lived at the time. Whether using organic material, metals or gemstones, every group of people, no matter what time, culture or civilization they belonged to, has relied on the same pieces of jewellery, and I find it thrilling to discover how they began, who wore them and what their cultural significance is, investigating their journey through the prism of different periods of lifestyle, fashion and artistic movements.

This is why I started my podcast in 2020, also called *If Jewels Could Talk*, in which I interview guests and experts about jewels ranging from Anne Boleyn's 'B' necklace to the poignant jewelled flower never completed by Peter Carl Fabergé as war and revolution raged in Russia. These conversations only sparked greater interest in the evolution and background of our most-worn designs, so I decided to take my research further and write this book.

I'm a big believer that small objects tell great stories, and so, in order to consider the significance of jewellery in more detail, I've identified the seven jewels that I think narrate our global human history. Within the timeline of each jewel lies a wealth of information about individual lives as well as our collective experience. From hoops and rings to beads and charms, brooches and cuffs to intricate head ornaments, the human stories these pieces generate reveal how they were valued and why they endured, and in doing so, unravel the universal symbols that link us to our past, present and future.

Not everyone is convinced by jewellery's important function in our lives; indeed, humans' need for adornment does seem inexplicable on the face of it, but I believe that, fundamentally, we wear jewellery *because* we are human.

Over the millennia, geography has changed, society has altered, people shift and move around the world, and yet what hasn't changed is the human aspiration for shelter, food, community, happiness and self-actualization. Given the state of the world over the past few years – with pandemics, climate change and political unrest – more and more people seem to be gravitating towards things that possess a deeper meaning. Jewellery has always fulfilled that role; from its genesis, it has conveyed feelings of comfort, peace and protection, as well as personally meaningful connections to loved ones. Increasingly, where we are born is not where we live, and jewels provide a tangible link with our memories of home and family. In our ever more frenetic society, there is an appealing quietness in the ritual of jewellery.

Whatever is occurring in the world, jewellery has always had a physical, emotional and spiritual hold over us. It's something we innately understand, maybe partly inherited through stories and learnt behaviours, as well as residing in the two linked strands twisting round each other like a chain that forms our DNA. Jewellery plays a part in our elusive search to keep fear at bay and feel whole, and there's no doubt we're attracted to the sense of permanence in a jewel, which lasts long after we have departed. In that way, at least we leave a mark on the world and something of ourselves behind. Objects can relay our story long into the future.

The book is an attempt to define what jewellery is, why we wear it and the profound meaning that humans have always attached to adorning themselves. And why, like the eternal circle of the hoop or ring, our need for jewellery never ends.

CHAPTER ONE

Hoops

I credit the humble hoop with being the world's first fashion accessory. Indeed, I'm convinced that, in the Book of Genesis, when the son of Abraham gives his fiancée a *shanf*, a golden earring, it would have been a hoop.

To talk about the history of hoops is to talk about the history of gold – the two are inextricably linked. Gold has played a role at every stage of human history; it has motivated entire civilizations and societies and driven men to endure intense hardship in the hope of discovering it. Ever since the third millennium, gold has been collected in particles eroded from rocks by panning riverbeds and streams. Open-cast and tunnel mining followed and then, many centuries later, that gold was transported from the 'New World'. Wherever it was found, a gold rush would ensue; indeed, on his first trip to America, the Italian explorer Christopher Columbus observed: 'O most excellent gold! Who has gold has a treasure that even helps souls to paradise.' In its natural state, gold is malleable, possessing a softness that makes it easy to manipulate. Once it was discovered that the gleaming brilliance of gold could be constructed into decorative shapes with simple tools, humans became particularly attached to the circle, an elemental shape that would have been visible everywhere in the natural world, in earth formations such as mounds and lakes to pebbles, fruits and shells. The circularity exhibited in nature became a guiding principle in human culture, emulated in art and jewellery, used in some way to make sense of the world around us.

Gold hoops are an identity marker, a golden signal of freedom and a direct link to ancestry. Plus, gold was a precious commodity for a status-exhibiting piece. The ancient peoples of the 2500 BCE African civilization in Nubia may have been the first to wear hoops, possibly as symbols of status and power within the community. The River Nile connected the Nubians to the Egyptians, and so the two civilizations shared strong trade links, as well as an understanding of the representational role that jewellery possessed in their cultures.

The hoop hasn't always been fashionable through the ages, and along the way there have been times when it faded into the background – during the European Middle Ages, for instance, when Renaissance hairstyles and high-necked fashions weren't very hoop-friendly. These were merely interludes, however, which never lasted long. The hoop always re-emerges, reimagined, blending into new environments and fashions, yet never changing shape. The continuous curved line of the hoop encircles us all.

THE FIRST HOOP

Since the invention of the wheel in the Bronze Age, circles have been linked to the ideas of eternity, rebirth and renewal. It was also a popular symbol in Celtic art, where the wheel's hub was believed to be the sun itself and the spokes the sun's shining rays.

Sicilians believed the wheel gave its owner protection from the greatest forces of nature, and the turning of the wheel was controlled by Fortuna, the Roman wheel goddess, who supervised the changing seasons and the fates of men; a goddess of good fortune it was best to keep on side.

Throughout 2,500 years of history, Sicily was invaded by the Greeks, Romans, Normans, Arabs and Spanish, each of whom left a cultural imprint on the island. As a result, every major civilization is visible in its Byzantine architecture, golden mosaics, dynamic traditions, folklore and the local craft of Sicily.

During the eighth century BCE, small, brightly painted donkey-drawn wagons were introduced to the Mediterranean island of Sicily from Greece, and these *carretto siciliano* trundled around the island, transporting produce. Following the fall of the Roman Empire, the Greek-style carts were mostly abandoned when the roads fell into disrepair, making the use of two-wheel vehicles impossible. Trade and transport were largely carried out by sea until the beginning of the nineteenth century, when the tradition of the carts was revived.

The carts were a complex construction. Firstly, a carver would craft the wooden parts in beech or walnut. A blacksmith would then provide the wrought-iron elements, such as highly embellished metal undercarriages and harnesses, before the *carradore* (wheelwright) finally assembled the pieces. The wood on the sides of these carts was often elaborately decorated with scenes from historical stories, chivalrous folk narratives and religious iconography, all daubed in bright colours. In this way, the carts carried Sicily's cultural history, traditions and folklore around like wandering picture-books, and in this way the epic stories of the island's past reached all its inhabitants.

The designer Domenico Dolce grew up in Sicily and recalled the carts moving around the island, and the traditional *carretto* wheels provided the inspiration for the Sicilian Cart hoops by Dolce & Gabbana, which revolve with a kaleidoscopic whorl of rubellite, amethyst, tourmaline, emerald and multicoloured sapphires and twelve gold filigree spokes. For him and Stefano Gabbana, the provenance and history of Sicily illustrated in the wheel earrings are as precious as the jewels themselves. Like the carts before them, the hoops shine with the memory of a culture in danger of being lost and forgotten.

QUEEN PU-ABI'S HOOPS

To be properly attired in Sumeria in ancient Mesopotamia (now southern Iraq), royalty and the elite members of society wore chokers and necklaces. We know this because, in December 1927, four years into an excavation of the city of Ur, the chief archaeologist Leonard Woolley unearthed the tomb of Queen Pu-abi, which had remained untouched for 4,500 years. The Queen lay on a wooden bier in the vaulted chamber, with her upper body entirely decorated with precious beads, pendants and chokers. Golden rings were found on each finger, and an intricately wrought leaf-and-flower ornament adorned her head. The quality of the ornaments was testament to the teams of skilled jewellers employed at the time in Ur. There were more beads and gold pendants, depicting plants and animals, and various vessels made from metal, stone and pottery dotted around the walls of the chamber.

The impressive quality and sheer quantity of jewels indicated status and prestige, but if there was any doubt about this woman's status, it was dispelled by the carved lapis lazuli cylindrical seals she was buried with. There were three of these pinned to her robe, but, as historians point out, one would have sufficed for personal identification – to boast this many was unusual. Possibly, she believed she needed them to underpin her authority when she presented herself to the gods in the afterlife. One of the seals included an engraving of a bunch of dates, which was a symbol of monarchy and the divine right to rule, whilst another was engraved with her name and the letters 'NIN', meaning lady or queen, thereby emphasizing her status and social influence. Scholars believe she ruled in her own right, since no husband is mentioned. Despite being only four feet tall, it was clear no other woman could have outshone Pu-abi in her radiant golden hair ornaments, headdresses of lapis lazuli, carnelian chokers and large gold hoop earrings.

The opulence of the grave goods wasn't the only reason the world took notice of Woolley's discovery. Queen Pu-abi's grave was discovered four years after King Tutankhamun's tomb, and it had been assumed until then that the entire region had been mostly ruled by men. Most women's seals at the time would have read 'wife of ... ', but Pu-abi's seal made no mention of her husband and showed no image of a king, indicating that she ruled the kingdom in her own right. This made her the first known female ruler in human history – and the first woman whose celebrated style was defined by powerful gold hoops.

Indeed, it's impossible to name a strong female

celebrity today who doesn't underpin their status with a pair of oversized gold hoops. Think of Rihanna, Madonna and J. Lo, to name but a few. Gold, being resistant to corrosion, survives from remote antiquity; even when it has been buried for centuries, it emerges into the sunlight with its magical sheen intact. Queen Pu-abi's lustrous hoops didn't corrode or tarnish and today shine with the same lustre as the day they were first created. Indeed, they'd look at home on the ears of Cardi B and Beyoncé today. Although separated by centuries, hoops worn by contemporary singers and celebrities measure a similar shoulder-dusting 8cm in diameter, like those found in the royal cemetery at Ur. Gold hoops are a jewel of eternity, and one could say Queen Pu-abi was an early trendsetter, who knew right from the off what a hoop could do for a woman.

EGYPTOMANIA

Contemporary reports of Pu-abi and Sumerian style disseminated and migrated out of Asia. Although there were limited sources of gold in the desert mines of Kush, by 1700 BCE, hoops were all the rage in Egypt. Everyone flaunted them: men, women, children – even cats, which were considered the most sacred of animals. The cat was associated with the goddess Bastet, daughter of the sun god Ra, who in turn was connected to music, dance, family, fertility and birth. A 2,500-year-old bronze sculpture of a cat, preserved in the Egyptian desert sands, was discovered with gold hoop earrings shining brightly on its ears.

The most popular form of earring was made up of several hollow triangular hoops soldered together. Gold was highly prized, evidenced by the pharaohs, who were believed to be living gods and titled 'the golden ones'. Gold embodied not only the warmth and light of the sun, but for the ancient Egyptians also represented the flesh of the sun god Ra, himself described as 'a mountain of gold' and with whom they hoped to be reunited in the afterlife. Golden hoops twisted with beads and faience were symbols of status, power and wealth for royals and pharaohs, as well as powerful queens such as Cleopatra and Nefertiti.

Egyptians suffered for the beauty of a hoop. Mummies that have been X-rayed show elongated and distended earlobes caused by the use of heavy ear ornaments. Some burial sites have revealed large metallic tubular hoops that had to be passed through an oversized piercing. Simple gold hoops, glass faience or semi-precious stones like jasper were worn by threading the open-ended hoop through the earlobe on a curve. And if you think the asymmetrical look is a modern trend, think again: Egyptians often wore two hoops in the one earlobe. Hoop earrings also drew the eye up towards intoxicating kohl-lined eyes and cheekbones, adding to the sense of seductive beauty.

Egyptian style has captured the modern imagination for

its opulence and exoticism, and we know that Egyptians, both men and women, went to great lengths over their appearance. All the accoutrements they used for their toilette are revealed as grave goods: combs, handheld mirrors, siltstone palettes to grind minerals such as the green malachite and galena (black kohl) they mixed with animal fats and oils to outline eyes, which were stored in beautiful calcite vessels. Crushed beetles and ochre were also combined with animal oils to create preferred shades of red lipstick.

As well as setting a certain standard of Egyptian beauty, practicality also played a part in the cosmetic routine. Recent scientific research demonstrates that the heavy use of kohl, a lead-based mineral, had anti-bacterial properties, which would have helped to combat water-borne eye infections common along the Nile River. Achieving a wing-tipped smoky eye wasn't simply about vanity, either, as kohl provided the benefit of reducing the dazzling glare from the desert sun.

Cleopatra wielded as much power as anyone in the ancient Mediterranean, ruling over one of its greatest king-doms, and she features in the line of strong and powerful women who were drawn to wear hoops as part of their day-to-day beauty arsenal. Taking into consideration that beauty standards do alter over time, coins minted during her reign portray the Queen with a jutting chin, curly hair and a large, aquiline nose, suggesting she was not a conventional beauty. Historians also draw attention to the ancient texts, none of which call the Egyptian Queen a beauty, instead praising her sharp wit and determination, as well as noting her excellent education. Cleopatra spoke seven languages and wrote philosophical treatises. Quite possibly the unflattering image that was engraved on coins and carved onto emeralds might have been a deliberate attempt to appear more masculine in order to survive and thrive in the patriarchal world she inhabited.

The image of another powerful Egyptian beauty was unveiled in 1912, when the now-famous painted bust of Nefertiti, currently housed in Berlin, was discovered. She was Queen of the 18th dynasty and, until her bust was revealed, was the little-known royal wife of Pharaoh Akhenaten as well as the probable stepmother of King Tutankhamun. The name Nefertiti means 'the beauty of the beautiful ones of the Aten, the beauty has come', and after the discovery of her bust, she became the poster girl for the ancient world almost overnight. She was depicted in this instance wearing large studs or plugs in her ears, but given that she ruled over the wealthiest period in ancient Egypt, I can't imagine the hoop didn't feature somewhere in her regime, and at least one renowned archaeologist believes that many of the ornate objects, including hoops, in the burial chamber of Tutankhamun were originally made for Nefertiti. Archaeologists are on the hunt for her tomb, and new technologies and height-ened interest worldwide make it more likely than ever that it will be found. There are so many more questions to be answered about the enduring enigma that was Nefertiti – not least her jewellery collection, which I hope would be just as splendid as Pu-abi's.

In 2017, Rihanna paid tribute to Nefertiti on the cover of *Vogue Arabia* by wearing saturated black eyeliner and golden disc earrings replete with turquoise beads, channelling Nefertiti's timeless allure. The fame and beauty of these fabled queens of the Nile has stretched deep into their afterlife, continuing to inspire styles even now.

TRIBAL HOOPS

The culture of hoops bowled out of Africa, along the Nile River, where the ancient Egyptians embraced the practice, and then on to Asia, where areas of Odisha in eastern India were populated by Africans. There are many tribes, each with its own way of dressing, distinctive forms of rituals and ways of honouring ancestors – but a jewellery culture is something they all share.

Large hoop earrings are an integral part of the traditional dress worn by the tribal communities of Gadaba, Bonda and Kondh in the eastern states of India. Kondh girls, for instance, are still recognizable by the three golden rings pierced through their noses, glass bead necklaces which drop to their hips and the large coin rings worn on fingers. From the moment of birth, the hoop plays an important role in the life of these women. Small bells swing from hoops on babies' ears to keep evil forces at bay, and noses and ears are pierced to provide an exit for any malign spirits that might penetrate the body's openings. A girl might have as many as sixteen golden hoops in one ear, combined with up to fifty hair clips and pins made of iron, copper and brass, creating a golden halo effect similar to Pu-abi.

Like Egyptian women's strained earlobes, the women of the Gadaba tribe appear to suffer for their efforts. Wearing jewellery is a strict social custom and is worn for the whole of a woman's life and not even removed for sleep. Gigantic swinging earrings are accompanied by smaller hoops, which embroider the edge of the ear and the lobe. Most astonishing are the eye-catching giant circular copper or wire earrings pushed through the cartilage of the ear, the weight of which is supported by a cord over the back of the head. The main hoop is so large it's easy to imagine a small child swirling them around their waist like a metallic hula hoop. Huge, silver, shoulder-brushing circlets like ear-chokers, redolent of Gadaba hoops, have been spotted on modern fashion runways. They make a seasonal splash but we don't share the strength of commitment of Gadaba women to support the ear heft – the hoop encumbrance might also interfere with mobile phone use – so, unlike their originators, they aren't for everyday wear.

In Bonda society, women enjoy a privileged position. This is seen in the marital norms of the community, with Bonda girls largely marrying boys who are at least five to ten years younger than them. The idea is that a woman looks after her husband as he grows up, and then, when he is older, he in turn cares for his wife. The hoops and rings worn by Bonda women are beautiful in their simplicity – but the whole bejewelled look includes wide anklets, delicate nose rings, armlets, thick neckbands and enormous hoop earrings. These customs remain robust today as tribes in India keep their unique style of jewellery intact. With the spread of globalization and more women choosing to study and work outside the village, however, customs are increasingly adapting to encompass a mix of modern and traditional dress.

The Romani are another tribal community strongly associated with gold hoops. An Indo-Aryan group who traditionally led a nomadic life, they originated from Rajasthan in northern India before migrating and spreading throughout Europe. Often called 'gypsies' because Europeans mistakenly thought they came from Egypt, historically the Romani wore yellow gold in the form of coins mounted as jewellery, since keeping their money close by and attached to their body made for a safe and portable 'purse'. These coin pendants and large hoops are a legacy of their Indian roots and connect the Romani people to their heritage.

Roma peoples are diverse, with a multitude of sub-ethnicities and languages throughout Europe, but even today their clothing and accessories express a sense of belonging to a community which is widespread. Gold and silver hoops embellish everything. Romani groups did not keep chronicles of their history, nor are there oral accounts. Instead, the custom of wearing hooped jewellery has passed down through generations of peoples with no homeland, and as such these hoops have become symbols worn to express identity and belonging. Over the years the fashion world has borrowed many elements from Roma culture, using the word 'gypsy' to conjure up a cultural stereotype of an exotic woman wearing a colourful headscarf, big hoop earrings and a long, flowing skirt, gazing into a crystal ball. This has made many of the young Roma diaspora feel misrepresented, and some are campaigning to have the word removed from the fashion industry's lexicon.

THE BRONZE AGE SHANNONGROVE GORGET

The discovery of metal working was an important stage in the development of the art of jewellery-making. Recently, a team of archaeologists published a report revealing that a hoard of Bronze Age artefacts recovered from a burial mound near Stonehenge were in fact the remains of a 3,800-year-old goldsmith's toolkit used for working gold. Microscopic analysis discovered gold traces on five of the stone tools with a similar composition to Bronze Age gold, and a detailed examination of tiny rubs and scratches revealed how they had been used to flatten, hammer and smooth sheets of gold, proving that the tools had shaped and manipulated gold in either liquid or metal form. The flint cups in the hoard may have been used to mix resins and adhesives, whilst the long sharp-end awl could have created perforations, patterns and representations of deities.

Ireland was rich in alluvial gold deposits during the Bronze Age, and the Shannongrove gorget is another early example of the hoop. This large, hammered, gold hooped collar was found in 1783, hidden in a peaty bog in Shannongrove, Limerick. Historians believe the holes underneath each circular terminal would have allowed a chain to run between them, passing by the back of the neck to complete the hoop. Most likely it was worn during ceremonies to denote rank. Society at this time was intensely hierarchical and status-conscious, and only royalty or members of the nobility would have worn gold.

Also called torcs or torques, these rigid circular neck-pieces embody some of the finest works of ancient Celtic art. Made from a wide, single piece of metal or narrower strands twisted together, the torque became an important symbol of power worn by leaders of both sexes. Indeed, Celtic artists often depicted deities wearing or holding such rings. The collars reflect sophisticated gold-working techniques with an elegant simplicity of design sometimes enhanced with subtle animal forms, floral motifs and geometric patterns such as parallel lines, chevrons, rope and circular shapes in gold wire.

Ancient writers noted that the first-century Celtic Queen Boudicca, who fought against the Romans in Britain, wore a gold neck ring in battle. This would have been worn to offer protection to the vulnerable throat and came to symbolize strength and bravery. The neckpiece was indestructible-looking and, residing at the front of the body, would have sent an immediate signal of potency to any advancing stranger: 'I am unbreakable' would have been the message.

The Roman army was initially daunted by the fearsome appearance of Boudicca. Although eventually defeated, she undoubtedly showed strength and spirit in rallying Britons to unite behind her and fight the tyranny and heavy taxes of Rome. The Gauls, whose elite warriors were richly adorned with gold necklaces and armbands, were also conquered by the Romans. Their military *armillae* armband decorations were modelled on Celtic gorgets. The tradition might have been started by the politician and general of the Roman Republic Titus Manlius, who accepted the challenge of single combat from one warrior whilst fighting the Gauls during the Battle of the Anio River and, upon killing his opponent, stripped the corpse of the torque and placed it around his own neck as a trophy.

As the torque was the Celtic symbol of authority, by his action Manlius earned the agnomen 'Torquatus'. In effect, by removing the Gaul's torque, he had taken the vanquished chieftain's strength for his own. The jewel in turn became a potent and visible token of Roman domination and, as such, over time the torque and also the armilla were adopted as official awards for valour, expressing the military might and strength of their soldiers.

It wasn't just the Celts and Romans who were part of an elite tradition of wearing hooped collars. Viking collars were mostly made in silver, due to limited gold sources, and they were fashioned like twisted circular rods. Although their neck hoops were slenderer-looking than the Celtic gorget, the Vikings layered them; the wealthier you became, the more torques you added to your neck. Like the Romani, the Vikings also used jewellery as ornamental currency, and the silver torques could be relied upon wherever they travelled. The quality and purity of the metal was easily tested by cutting a small nick in the silver, and this provided much-needed flexibility for a mobile group like the Vikings, who used the silver collars to trade over vast distances from Scandinavia, Britain and Russia. Most economies accepted silver, so there was no need to worry about getting by on long voyages. You could call silver the Viking euro, eliminating as it did the need for different currencies. From Baghdad, the Vikings also brought back Islamic dirham coins, which they sometimes strung on necklaces worn as badges of honour, impressing a connection with foreign lands. Just as there is a roaring trade nowadays in counterfeit luxury items such as Chanel handbags and Rolex watches, traders began selling fake dirhams, complete with pseudo-Arabic inscriptions. Swinging with dirhams or not, however, silver torques served to strengthen an individual's personal value in the Vikings' culture of honour.

I often see contemporary incarnations of the torque shape in Scandinavian design, inherited from the Viking age. Recently, in Paris, Francesca Amfitheatrof, artistic director of Louis Vuitton, was inspired by the gorget to create Le Royaume, a massive, articulated collar with a large sapphire held within a white gold and diamond grid, reminiscent of chain mail, to protect the neck. Many of her pieces share the aesthetic properties of armour, a glittering metaphor for Celtic confidence and determination. Two phoenix wings encircle the neck suspending a 65.26-carat tsavorite garnet, whilst another is worked into the shape of a gorget bandana engraved with trefoils, chevrons and V-shapes, echoing metallic design patterns of the Bronze Age goldsmiths. The metal mesh of the throat-covering is soft and fluid, so won't offer the defence of a traditional Bronze Age collar, but with its $124,000 price tag it definitely draws attention to individuality and financial status, if not prowess on the battlefield.

POMANDER HOOPS

As we know only too well from our recent experience of the Covid-19 pandemic, when people travel and mix, they share more than just cultural practices, goods and artistic customs; they also distribute disease and viruses. The first recorded pandemic was the Justinian Plague in the sixth century, and over the next 200 years of resurgence it killed millions of people across the globe. It's widely believed that infectious diseases such as leprosy and smallpox travelled along the Silk Road, the network of paths that connected China with Europe used from the second century BCE to export goods such as silk, spices, precious metals, minerals, handicrafts and paintings. Although we may now be confident about the origins and spread of contagions, however, our ancestors weren't so sure. During the Middle Ages they believed disease was a manifestation of the wrath of God, the curse of the Devil or even the consequence of fetid, bad-smelling air.

You might well have caught the pleasant aroma of baking bread or smoke from a wood fire from time to time, but personal sanitation was rare during the Middle Ages, and the air was usually pervaded by a fetid stench of sweat, urine and body grime. Conditions were so bad that city dwellers resorted to wearing a type of wooden clog over their shoes to raise them above the human excrement running through the gutters and the rotting animal entrails slung out by slaughterhouses. There was a belief at the time that such foul smells harboured particles of disease, so people started carrying sweet-smelling herbs wherever they went in the hopes of overcoming these dangerous miasmas.

The name 'pomander' is derived from the French term *pomme d'ambre*, meaning 'apple of amber' and is essentially a ball assembled from various fragrant herbs and scents. There was a recipe for making pomander included in John Partridge's *Treasury of Commodious Conceits and Hidden Secrets*, published in London in 1586. A mixture of sticky resins from tree bark and rose shrubs were ground into a powder, dissolved in rosewater and heated. Removed from the fire, the mixture was coated with sweet-smelling cinnamon and cloves before being kneaded into the shape of an apple, which was then rolled through grains of dissolved ambergris, deer musk and civet musk. The potent concoction was blended before a hole was made in the 'apple', which would be ready to hang. The word pomander describes both the therapeutic preparation as well as the decorative metallic container, which swung like a herbal amulet from hoops attached to neck chains or a belt or girdle at the waist. When placed in the brass, silver or gold spherical cages, the idea was that the perforations in the container would allow the protective perfume to seep out and disperse, defeating disease. You could say pomanders were an early decorative PPE of sorts.

The silver-gilt pomander belonging to Mary, Queen of Scots was hinged at the base, allowing it to open into eight segments, so she could fill each one with a different scent. Her cousin, Queen Elizabeth I, was frequently painted wearing her pomander, which had a hoop at each end so she could incorporate it into her rosary as a pendant on the end of the chain. In this way she hoped to enhance the efficacy of the scent with prayer. Others at the time embellished pomanders with gemstones, pearls, sapphires, diamonds, rock crystals, emeralds and amethysts, believing that the talismanic power of 'magical' stones would aid the protective work of the pomander.

By the eighteenth century, the pomander had morphed into an orange studded with cloves and other spices to sweeten the surrounding air, something that survives in modern times as a ritualistic holiday pastime. As we know, the pomander wasn't brought back into action as one of the front-line defences against the spread of infection during the recent Covid-19 pandemic, instead we relied on face masks and self-test kits, all of which produced tons of discarded plastic globally. Brazilian designer Sebastian Jaramillo has responded to this waste crisis by recycling the plastic from Covid kits, old pens, toothbrushes and plastic cases into contemporary hoop earrings. He grinds the plastic before placing it in the oven to form a solid block, which, when cooled, he then carves into the desired hoop shape. The resulting material looks like dramatic rock crystal. His next project? Cleaning up vape cigarette filters from the beaches, collecting around 35–40 butts for a single earring.

Hoops for Elizabethan men

There was a time when the most luxurious item to swing from a hoop was a natural pearl. During the sixteenth and seventeenth centuries, there was a fashion amongst wealthy men to wear a pearl in one ear as a sign of courtly swagger and bravado. In 1577, the British history compendium *Holinshed's Chronicles* described pearl earrings being worn by 'lusty courtiers also and gentlemen of courage'. An earlier fashionable moment for male hoops was during the Roman Empire, when renowned general, politician and writer Julius Caesar wore hoops to show strength and solidarity with the men in his army, who wore hoop earrings into battle.

Whilst Queen Elizabeth I swung her pomander, England's greatest poet and playwright William Shakespeare, of whom she was a great fan, wore a small hoop in his ear. One of the most famous portraits believed to be Shakespeare, known as the Chandos portrait, which resides in London's National Portrait Gallery, shows him wearing a single small gold hoop. Just across the gallery on the opposite wall hangs a portrait of the gallant Sir Walter Raleigh, who posed decked out in a silk doublet with pearl buttons, a fur-lined coat and one large, shimmering pearl hanging from a hoop earring. Raleigh is described as a Renaissance man – a poet, explorer, soldier, sailor, courtier and personal favourite of Queen Elizabeth I. The earring in his portrait delivered a message to the Queen: at the time, pearls were symbols of virginity, which would directly relate to the reputation of the 'Virgin Queen', thereby symbolizing his loyalty.

It was common for seamen like Raleigh to sport earrings as a sign of their travels; gold hoops made fine examples of the chic of the exotic acquired on a swashbuckling adventure. Legend stated that young sailors were given hoops to commemorate their first treacherous crossing of the southernmost tip around the Cape of Good Hope. Some believed a pierced ear would cure seasickness, whereas another widely held belief was that earrings were worn to make a down payment on a burial if the sailor died far away from home. This is a folklore story believed to be true by the actor Morgan Freeman, who spoke about his gold hoops on Instagram. His inspiration to wear them, he says, came from the 'old-fashioned sailor culture', as they would be 'worth just enough for someone to buy him a coffin in case he died unexpectedly in a random place'. 'That's why sailors used to wear them,' he added.

King Charles I took to the fashion from a young age, wearing one large pearl earring until his death. He debuted a teardrop-shaped pearl resting on a gold crown topped with an orb and cross when he was just fifteen years old. An unpopular boy who suffered from acute shyness and a stammer, perhaps felt the pearl would give him the confidence he sadly lacked and provide the antidote to his short stature. Natural pearls in particular, the rarest gemstone, were the King's favourite. The hooped pearl appeared in every Van Dyck and Rubens portrait of him, worn on his left ear, and became synonymous with the image of the romantic cavalier that he wished to portray. When he was found guilty of high treason by Oliver Cromwell, he went to the scaffold wearing the pearl earring as he placed his neck on the executioner's block.

Hoops – then and now – are shorthand to signify an adventurous and unconventional spirit. The stereotypical image of a pirate on the high seas has him bedecked in drilled gold coins and hoops. During the golden age of piracy in the seventeenth and eighteenth centuries, much of Europe had a number of sumptuary laws in place that regulated people's attire, prescribing what colours people could wear and controlling who could sport jewellery. Men weren't allowed to wear jewels, and anyone who refused to obey these laws could face a heavy fine or even jail. Flamboyant pirate dress and gold jewels may well have been a direct response to these laws, making their earrings a symbol of rebellion and a subversive choice to flout rules.

CREOLE HOOPS

Roughly 100 years after Sir Walter Raleigh was leading expeditions to the Americas, the term Creole emerged in the early days of colonial expansion in New Orleans to identify descendants of French, Spanish and Portuguese settlers living in the West Indies and Latin America. Basically, being born and raised in the colonies was what made people Creole. They were descendants of African or mixed heritage parents, as well as progenies of the first French and Spanish Europeans. Historically, it's described as a place-based ethnicity. People of any race could identify as Creoles, and during the 1700s most people in New Orleans were Creole.

Creole hoops aren't completely circular, but slightly elongated in shape, with a wide base and tapered sides to the top. In New Orleans, Creole hoops are considered a folk tradition which is passed down through each generation as a rite of passage. Large Creole hoops have become more than a fashion to young women; they are a cultural statement and a visible sign of reaching maturity and a certain station in life. Girls' ears are pierced at birth, and they are given larger-sized Creole earrings as they mature.

The elongated shape of Creole hoops could have been inspired by the African Fulani people, who were forcibly expatriated to America during the slave trade. They came from several parts of West Africa, where they lived a nomadic and pastoral life observing Islamic religious practices. Fulani women adorn themselves with all kinds of jewellery, including *kwottone kanye* (the Fulani) term for earrings), rings, bangles and necklaces. The shape of their earrings is remarkably similar to the Creoles', including a unique twist in the hoop, which in the native Fulani language is called *bhoylé*. For centuries, royal women wore these hoops in solid gold as a sign of nobility, and it was customary for women of status to wear larger earrings, which could be up to a massive 15cm long. To the Fulani women, jewellery expressed strength, and the hoops were used as a form of portable wealth to pass down to children.

The children born to the first African slaves brought to Louisiana were called 'black Creoles'. Uprooted from their original homes and stripped of clothes for the crossing, slavers would aim to remove any tangible connection with their identity, culture and home, and although in some cases beads or coral were permitted, jewellery became a potent means of controlling enslaved groups. This propelled Creoles to develop elements of their heritage, including jewellery, to maintain a sense of their cultural norms. For many Creoles, earrings were an expression of their African ancestry.

Carmen Miranda went to the US from Brazil and introduced an entirely new look to the world inspired by the outfits worn by Afro-Brazilian street vendors. Baianas women from north-east Brazil wore white lace tops, gold hoops and shiny accessories with simple cloth turbans as they carried trays of fruit on their head. These female icons of Bahia had ancestors who had arrived as slaves from Africa, and their hoops were a way of celebrating their legacy, subsequent liberation and economic independence. In one of her early films, *Banana da Terra*, Miranda wore a costume mimicking the look of these street sellers, and Tropicalia costume became an overnight sensation.

The cultural roots of her look, including the hoops she wore, were associated with poor black women, so a Portuguese-born film star adopting the dress of a racially marked persona wasn't without controversy. At the time, however, she chimed with the prevailing fashion for Afro-Brazilian culture, particularly samba, tango and habanera music. This was encouraged by Brazilian

President Getúlio Vargas, who saw it as a policy aimed at creating a sense of national identity that embraced the black population. Some Brazilians had mixed feelings about the way that their culture was presented, but there is no doubt it kickstarted a Tropicalismo movement that was fashionable all over the world, which in turn drew attention to a hitherto marginalized people back home.

As for Miranda, she may have been forever typecast by her costume, but 'the Brazilian Bombshell' became the highest paid actress in Hollywood and was the first Latin American to be honoured with a star on Hollywood's Walk of Fame.

Today, Carmen's style survives in fashion and popular culture; the combination of lace frills, floral brooches and fruity headpieces creates a bold vivacity and a sense of rhythm and exoticism wherever they are deployed. Despite the controversy, the hoops Carmen wore can be seen as part of creating a sense of unity integral to dress and identity, shaping a modern idea of shared cultural practices.

Even seventy years after her death, people still respond to her image and marketing teams and fashion journalists alike echo her 'tropical' Latin look in designs and on the pages of magazines. Not a season goes by without some sort of reworking of her signature look on a runway.

FRIDA MANIA

Arguably no one has done more to afford the humble hoop its legendary status in popular culture than the Mexican artist Frida Kahlo. The world has an eternal fascination with her life story: the pain and suffering she endured from a permanent disability after contracting polio as a child, a near fatal bus accident, several miscarriages and a tortured love story with her husband, the muralist Diego Rivera. The portrayal of her body wracked with pain became a recurring feature in her art and yet Kahlo countered her frailty by threading flowers through her hair with golden hoops shining below, draping her torso with Colombian jade, wearing weighty silver bangles and piling fingers with massive rings. In a way her jewels armed her against the pain, forming part of the strength and power she presented to the world. The look she created for herself was important, as she wrote to her mother from San Francisco in 1930: 'The gringas really like me a lot and pay close attention to all the dresses and rebozos [shawls] that I brought with me, their jaws drop at the sight of my jade necklaces.'

Mexico had been a colony of Spain for nearly 300 years, and craftsmen arrived in the country producing gold and silver jewellery using European techniques like filigree, fine wirework formed into delicate tracery, which is the type of ornamental earring Kahlo illustrated in her paintings. And she favoured silver hoops like those made in Taxco, Mexico, known for its silver mining. She often designed her own jewellery; her pre-Colombian jade beads represented in paint in *Self-Portrait With Necklace* may have originated from an excavated Mayan site in south-eastern Mexico and were strung together by Frida.

Largely, it was the brooding gaze, signature floral Tehuana coiffure, monobrow, gold earrings and red lips depicted in numerous self-portraits that led her to become one of the most recognized women of the twentieth century. Kahlo's strong personal identity still captivates new generations and, like Carmen Miranda, is endlessly emulated. Recently, one self-portrait, *Diego and I*, was sold for a record-breaking $34.9 million, becoming the most expensive artwork ever bought at auction. Her indelible image adorns tote bags, T-shirts, trainers, cosmetics, tequila and countless other fashion items. Her appearance is familiar around the globe and endures in its originality.

Frida's work is filled with symbolism that references the traumas of her life, as well as the iconographies and philosophies that interested her, especially in her home country, where she led the charge for a modern, independent Mexico. Kahlo was also a champion of her homeland's indigenous customs. She wore flamboyant Mexican folk dresses, colourful shawls and pre-Colombian jewellery as a performative display of her identity. The jewellery she chose was always visible in portraits and photographs, striking a personal note. The golden Spanish chandeliers and hoops she wore had a dual purpose – to draw the eyes of onlookers to focus on her face, as well as highlight the beauty of Mexican culture and crafts.

HOOPS IN MUSIC

The American-born French singer, actress and icon of the jazz age Josephine Baker had a significant role in promoting the hoop. In 1929, she was photographed nude for *Vanity Fair* by George Hoyningen-Huene, wearing nothing but a strategically placed piece of fabric and holding a long strand of pearls. The lighting of the monochrome portrait draws the eye to her face, which is framed by a giant pair of golden hoops, dropping so low they almost brush against three lacquer neckpieces. The necklaces were created by artist Jean Dunand and decorated with an abstract pattern mimicking African textiles. He had been inspired by the South African Ndebele women, who used stacks of rings to exaggerate their necks as a sign of feminine beauty. The glint of the hoops was subtle in the sepia-style photograph, but made a proud statement nonetheless.

At one time the highest paid performer in Paris, Baker became a courageous member of the resistance in the 1940s, infiltrating the Nazi Party and feeding back information to her confidants in Paris by writing messages on sheet music. Following the liberation of Paris, she was awarded the Croix de Guerre and the nation's highest award, the Legion of Honour. After the war she returned to the US to use her status as a war hero to bring attention to racial inequality. Baker's mother was part black and Apalachee Indian, whilst her father was a black Spaniard, and she had felt the impact of racism acutely. Her hoops became emblems of identity and female power amongst African American women.

Hoops have since become synonymous with certain music scenes. They featured prominently in New York's urban disco period and later became swinging stars of the pop and hip hop movements, as well as in rap and R&B circles. Hoops play a central role in the lives and pride of working-class African American and Latina women and swing with a currency symbolic of these women's culture and ancestry.

The first versions of bold, door-knocker-sized hoop earrings arrived in the 1980s. These hoops weren't made of precious metal; they were hollow, and some were sold for just a few dollars in stores across America, but they were an instant style hit for women of colour. These oversized ear girdles came to be known as 'bamboos', proclaiming African and Caribbean flair whilst making women feel connected to their roots. The fashion of the large bamboos was enabled by the fact that they could be made hollow and therefore light. Hip hop stars like MC Lyte, Roxanne Shanté and Salt-N-Pepa wanted 'big-ass' earrings to wear in music videos, and these hoops were also taken up by trans women and nonbinary femme dancers of New York's underground ballroom scene.

Hoops then got political and became a charged accessory for activism and a surging female political voice. Once one of the most powerful identity markers for women of colour, hoops became the subject of intense debate around cultural appropriation when white women started wearing them and they were reinvented as 'fashionable' by white designers for the runway shows. When the legendary costume designer Patricia Field, who dressed actress Sarah Jessica Parker in the TV series *Sex and the City*, put her character in a pair of door-knocker hoop earrings, legions of the show's fans immediately took to hoops for an edgy and hip look. Pretty soon a meme was launched: 'White girls, take off your hoops'. The late André Leon Talley, a contributing editor for American *Vogue*, sought to calm the argument. 'The hoop earring is a beautiful ethnic symbol,' he said. 'It does not belong to black women but is a part of black culture'.

In the twenty-first century, cultural appropriation is an inevitable consequence of globalization and yet it can have a positive effect. Creativity relies on the exchange of ideas, styles and traditions, which is one of the interesting aspects of a modern, multicultural society. However, it is important to show appreciation for customs and to give credit to their origins.

Today, hoops are bigger than ever before. 'They call me Cardi Bardi, banging body, spicy mami, hot tamale,' raps Cardi B in her hit 'I Like It'. In the video for the song she is dressed in a lemon-yellow ruffle skirt, a silken headscarf and gigantic gold hoops, it's a show-stopping look that reclaims her roots as an American Hispanic woman and is confirmation that hoops will always be an eye-catching shorthand for culture, heritage and power.

Nose rings

Throughout history, piercing has waxed and waned with the customs and fashions of the time. In the thirteenth century, the Catholic Church banned ear piercing, claiming that it was unduly altering one's appearance as created by God. As a result, piercings were driven into counterculture as a high-risk activity, becoming a signal of rebellion in the West for the next few centuries. This wasn't the case in Africa and Asia, where piercing wasn't purely for decorative reasons, but also served magical purposes. Specifically, a piercing provided an exit route for any evil spirit or malign energy. The Berber and Beja tribes of Africa gift gold nose jewellery to their future wives to this day, the size and value of the pieces attesting to the wealth of the family.

In India, nose piercings are as much a custom as bangles or a bindi. Some believe the tradition dates as far back as the first century, whereas others believe the practice arrived with the Mughals from Central Asia during the 1500s. The goddess Parvati, the wife of the Hindu god Shiva, wears a nose ring, which is symbolic of her marriage. One of her most famous forms is as the goddess

Kanyakumari, whose temple is at the southernmost tip of India. Legend has it that she remains in the form due to broken marriage promises, and her diamond nose piercing is said to sparkle so brightly that it is visible even from the sea. Today, some women opt for a simple stud or ring to wear every day, but for weddings and religious ceremonies, they might be replaced by the Maharashtrian *nath*, the North Indian *latkan* or *nathani*, large hoops decorated with precious gems and supported with an embellished chain. In certain Himalayan states the septum piercing is adorned with a *bulak*, a hooped ornament that sits snug to the nose or hangs delicately just above the upper lip. It's also a look that's been spotted on stars including Rihanna, FKA twigs and Zoë Kravitz.

Piercing in the West hit the mainstream when hippies returned from India and brought the tradition with them. In 1968, *Time* magazine credited the foundation of the hippie movement with historical precedent as far back as the *sadhu* of India, the spiritual seekers who had renounced the worldly life. Most hippies rejected mainstream organized religion in favour of a more personal spiritual experience, though many resonated with Eastern religions like Buddhism and Hinduism as they were seen as less rule-bound and more inclined to do away with materialistic baggage.

Nose piercings became popular during the punk movement of the 1970s, when they were used as a sign of rebellion against the status quo. Punks railed against a certain type of formality, which disappeared forever when the revolution began in London, smashing its way into fashion and art and creating a worldwide ruckus that redefined what was thought of as a jewel. Now, any type of sharp object could be pushed through earlobes – the more menacing-looking the better – and metallic hoops were replaced by long, utilitarian-style safety pins. British punk rockers were the ultimate exponents of anarchy, and Johnny Rotten, a member of the Sex Pistols, was known to wear safety pins in his ears and across jackets and shirts.

Gradually there was a process of legitimization for the piercing. Hard-edged nose rings progressed into things of gentler beauty. Piercings prettied themselves up as tiny holes punctuating ear lobes twinkled with diamond hoops. Ear curation became the new form of styling. Elaborate hoops crept up models' ears on the Givenchy and Chanel runways and those of activists pictured on the cover of *British Vogue*, whilst the model Daria Werbowy showed off her myriad gold rings in her upper ears in Celine advertising campaigns. No part of an ear is now viewed as out of bounds, and it's common to see multiple piercings in the cartilage of the upper ear and septum and constellations of twinkling hoops in the curves and whorls of the ear. Piercings have the potential to be transformative, but they can also be addictive. The fashion crowd get competitive, and some have up to sixteen piercings in one ear – much like the Gadaba tribe in Africa.

We're also seeing a renaissance in male ear piercing. When Harry Styles arrived at the Met Gala in New York a few seasons ago wearing shimmery Gucci with one pearl hoop hanging in his right ear, he was perhaps unknowingly channelling Sir Walter Raleigh. In fact, the first recorded male piercing was on Ötzi, a 5,500-year-old mummified iceman who was discovered in 1991 lying face down on the edge of a glacier in the Alps, with his ear piercing still intact. During the ninth century BCE, stone reliefs in Iraq portrayed men with pierced ears, and even scrolling back to Ur during Queen Pu-abi's reign, small hoops, most likely for piercings, were documented as grave goods.

Ultimately, however, there's a question mark over whether piercing can retain its subversive reputation. It's morphed into being too pretty to shock. It's still a youthful thing – models, activists and actresses continue to boast their latest piercings, witnessed by Gigi Hadid's septum piercing making a *Vogue* headline – and yet from its anarchic years of pirates and punk, getting a piercing has become a rite of passage for the midlife crisis. Mothers attend piercing parties with their daughters – Gwyneth Paltrow and her daughter Apple visit piercing pioneer Maria Tash in New York together. And yet no self-respecting punk rocker would have dressed like their mum.

At their core, piercings are an expression of each person's identity. The vogue for the glittering ear will endure – maybe, until there's no space left. Then the next generation of rebellious spirits will find a new area to pierce to make their own edgy and eloquent statement.

When the world locked down and we socialized via Zoom calls and FaceTime, hoops became the Covid accessory. They provided just enough glint and glamour to light the face, à la Cleopatra, whilst elevating lockdown loungewear. An arresting earring invariably makes an impact and hoops struck the perfect note of understated elegance. Girls everywhere went online in pursuit of the optimal hoop, causing sales to spike. The unprecedented period of slowing down has given most the time to evaluate what we actually need – and wear – on a daily basis, and the concept of seasonal trends feels increasingly alien. Fashion influencers, including Hailey Bieber and Bella Hadid, told *Vogue* that hoops were the one accessory they couldn't live without during lockdown, advising readers to eschew fussy frippery in favour of gold hoops to add a point of interest to our increasingly similar grey athleisure outfits.

Hoops are one way to express your individuality, but they are also an enduring symbol of unity. They connect us to the origins of humanity, a tradition that dates further back than any of us really know. Throughout history they have retained their iconic status as a symbol of power and identity. The story of the hoop continues. Recently, twisted, mismatched and knotted hoops have been trending. Times may change, but fresh styles will appear with a new vitality. It's the simple magic of hoop design: it invariably comes full circle.

CHAPTER TWO

RINGS

Rings have been supercharged with the symbolism of love for around 4,000 years. They act as visual celebrations of important milestones in our lives, commemorating birth, betrothal, friendship and mourning. We are arguably emotionally connected to rings more than other forms of jewellery because they are traditionally associated with solidifying bonds between individuals. People who don't wear jewellery much will still usually wear a ring. More than any other jewel, rings represent declarations of love, loyalty and trust. Even in prehistory, rings fashioned out of braided reeds, hemp or mammoth bone were used by our ancestors to identify the person with whom their life was shared. In time, they were upgraded to iron, but whatever the material, rings have always been used to pledge a long-term commitment – be it love, marriage, a promise, an oath or even a reminder of the eternity of death.

For Vikings, rings served as a symbol of oaths and promises, the circular ring shape representing reciprocity and commitment. Rings were also a constant reminder of obligation and oaths they had taken and promised. The pharaohs in ancient Egypt first wore rings as amulets, signifying eternity and brokering contracts between mortals and gods. Their rings often featured motifs such as vipers, scorpions and scarabs in lapis lazuli or turquoise, as symbols of rebirth, resurrection and immortality.

Rings have always been the jewels that have enabled people to exercise trust between one another. They are personal stories at our fingertips and, in a wider sense, they make lasting artifacts that tell us who we are as a people – both societally and individually.

TOE RINGS

Whenever summer approaches, we might start thinking about getting our feet 'beach ready'. Maybe we'll give ourselves a pedicure or pretty-up our bare feet with a colourful beaded anklet or silver toe ring. But toe rings aren't just a hot summer trend; just ask Hornedjitef, a 2,200-year-old Egyptian priest, whose mummified remains now reside in the British Museum. He was buried with a thick gold ring on the big toe of his left foot. This wasn't uncommon in ancient Egypt. Legs and feet were feted for their ability to move people through life's journey and into the afterlife. Indeed, the set of funerary jewellery made for one of Pharaoh Thutmose III's wives contained gifts including gold sandals and toe stalls (golden covers to prevent toes falling off during the embalming process), designed to protect her and transport her safely into the afterlife. So important was it to ancient Egyptians to propel the dead to eternity by keeping the foot intact that Tutankhamun was buried with forty-two golden pairs of sandals and toe stalls.

But it wasn't just Egyptian royalty whose toes were encircled by jewellery. Around ten years ago, archaeologists discovered two ancient Egyptian skeletons, dating back more than 3,300 years, both buried with toe rings made of copper alloy. Unlike the toe stalls in Tutankhamun's tomb, these rings were likely to have been worn whilst the individuals were still alive. The skeleton of one of the men showed several fractures, including his right femur, which had set at an angle and must have caused considerable pain during his life. A metal toe ring was looped around the toe of this foot, which indicated to the archaeologists that it might have been used for healing purposes. The act of 'binding' or 'encircling' was a powerful magical device used in ancient Egypt, and I know many people today who find that a tightly fitted copper bangle helps with joint aches and pains in their wrist, so perhaps the copper toe ring performed the same function in ancient Egypt. Some metaphysical healers use copper to treat the circulatory system by stimulating the metabolic process to encourage healing.

Indian toe rings are also believed to possess a reflexology benefit. They tend to be worn on the upper part of the second toe, between the nail and first joint, and by pressing on a nerve, these toe rings, or *bichiya*, are thought to keep the body in balance. They have an ancient history that may have originated in the Vedic period, around 1500–800 BCE, and the Vedas (ancient Hindu texts) refer to the practice of women wearing toe rings as a symbol of marriage and femininity. Ornate silver toe rings are worn in pairs on the second toe of each foot and carry a social significance for married women in the Hindu culture. There are *bichiya* sets that have pairs for four toes, leaving only the small toe unadorned. Ornate and delicate, the silver rings are placed by the husband on his wife's toes during the wedding ceremony. Gold is considered the metal of the gods, symbolizing Lakshmi, the goddess of wealth, and is therefore believed to be inappropriate worn below the waist. According to the ancient healing science of Ayurveda, silver toe rings absorb a woman's positive energy from the earth and transfer it to the wearer. Also, they were traditionally thought to hold positive acupressure benefits on the nerves of the toe leading to the female reproductive organs.

Signet rings

At a time in history when most people didn't read or write, signet rings played an essential role. A personalized seal of clay, agate, carnelian or gypsum would be lightly pressed on wax to act as a signature and make a document legally binding. These distinctive or distinguishing marks on the ring were the equivalent of modern-day written signatures and functioned as marks of authority and ownership. The imagery and text were carved in reverse so that when the ring was pressed into wax, the resulting image would appear the right way round.

In ancient Egypt these rings were viewed as badges of high administrative rank. In the tomb relief at Amarna, Akhenaten and his wife Nefertiti are depicted at the window of royal appearances (the architectural element associated with the religious and administrative duties of the royal couple) throwing signet rings down to his official Ay and his wife, rewarding them for their service.

Later, signet rings played an important role in Roman life. The wealth of the Romans attracted the best glyptic artists, and signet rings became increasingly large. Gemstones were engraved with animals, such as the heron, associated with vigilance, or the boar, which was venerated for its warrior-like attributes. Mythological and historical events were also popular features, as were portraits of poets, philosophers and military rulers. Emperor Augustus sealed documents with his own portrait, as did his successors and plenty of private individuals too. You could say these were early Roman versions of 'selfies', created to bear witness to their individualism and success in life. Images boasted of the pleasures of drinking, and even their mistresses were depicted in the nude or engaged in sexual intercourse, like an ancient form of pornography.

Whilst mostly worn by men, during the Byzantine period women also began to wear signet rings donned with their family crests. Women were starting to be recognized as the caretakers of their households and their families' possessions and so would need signet rings for 'sealing', which meant locking things that had to be kept safe in the house. Their rings might also be required to act as a personal signature.

As the centuries went by, signet rings increasingly became objects of status used not merely as a signature, but to impress the wealth and heritage of nobles and knights upon others. Heraldry in the form of coats of arms, crests and badges became a theme. The owner's coat of arms was typically painted in brilliant colours and set on the ring beneath a crystal intaglio. These rings were also good for business. The growing merchant class wore them to sign documents and mark goods and shipments, making it easier to identify goods on arrival and authenticate documents to prevent forgeries and theft.

It was during the eighteenth and nineteenth centuries that signet rings became fashionable and popular objects for gentlemen collectors. Although their function was being rapidly replaced by the adhesive envelope and written signatures, signet rings continued to be worn mainly as proof of family lineage. Crests which were once emblazoned on the shields of knights in shining armour became a symbolic way to represent an ancestral family name. They were regarded as the mark of a well-dressed gentleman and were worn to show off proof of pedigree and exalted bloodline. This was particularly true for the young men who went on their Grand Tour. The 2nd Duke of Devonshire's Grand Tour took two years, during which time he collected medals, coins and Roman, Greek and Renaissance carved gems in rings and on his return housed them in his stately home, Chatsworth House in Derbyshire, where his collection of 500 carved gems is displayed to this day. Trays of the miniature sculptures show complicated classical tales carved into sardonyx, sapphire, carnelian, aquamarine and amethyst. The Duke understood the stories being illustrated and would invite people with a similar interest in scholarly studies to come and enjoy the gems in the signet rings, together delving into the stories using texts and portraits. A whole world was based around the stones, and he communicated his passion for these items of jewellery to others. Only the most privileged men and women with classical tastes could acquire the magnificent hardstone gems, because demand for them was so great.

Many years ago, I wrote in *Tatler* magazine that men should melt their signet rings down and have them made into chains, because they were old-fashioned and smacked of elitism. This was ahead of the later fashion, propelled by actor Paul Mescal in the BBC series *Normal People*, for male chains. In fact, jewellery designers came to the rescue, creating chic signet alternatives, renamed 'pinkie' rings, with flat, shield-shape tops that are free from the pomp of any heraldic symbolism. Maybe I shouldn't have judged the signet so harshly, as the Latin family mottoes engraved beneath a crest can act as a call to action, or something to try to live up to at least. *Forti Nihil Difficile* – 'nothing is impossible for the brave' – couldn't help but inspire you through the day, and *Ich Dien* ('I serve') is the German motto inscribed underneath a crest of golden ostrich feathers on the King's signet ring, reminding him daily of his duty to his subjects.

BETROTHAL RINGS

Since rings were customary to mark a business agreement, it made sense that they were used in ancient Rome to 'seal' a marriage contract. These iron rings were called *annulus pronubus* and served as public markers approved by the early Christian Church that a contract had been made between the couple, as well as between their families. The practice of wearing rings on the fourth finger of the left hand stems from the ancient belief that this particular digit contained the *vena amoris*, the vein leading directly to the heart. Many of us still adhere to that custom now.

Codes of marital behaviour were recorded in script

on 4,000-year-old clay tablets by the Sumerians in Mesopotamia, like early 'pre-nups', recommending what the couple should receive in terms of bridal gifts, oil, domestic utensils and silver. One ancient Assyrian marriage contract written in cuneiform script (one of the earliest systems of writing), which is on display at the Istanbul Archaeology Museums, even records the price to be paid by both parties should the marriage not work out: 'Laqipum must pay Hatala five minas of silver', and vice versa. The rings made a public pledge of their intentions and were exchanged as tokens between the bride and groom, the eternal circle symbolic of the intention that this be an unending union. Often rings were decorated with patterns, Hercules knots and inscriptions running between foliate sprays and sometimes even featured portraits of the happy couple. In some cases, the rings were believed to possess amuletic values for protection and procreation, without which a marriage was considered unsuccessful and could be dissolved.

Although synonymous with engagements today, diamond-set rings dating back to Medieval Europe have been found that contain inscriptions that declare love, and a priest's manual written by Guillaume Durand during the thirteenth century confirmed the symbolic importance of the use of diamonds in wedding rings:

A certain sage, Proteus, seeking a sign of love, made a ring of iron and mounted a diamond in it, and in this way, brides could be identified as married, since, as iron tames, so love conquers all men, for there is nothing more insistent than love's passion. And as a diamond is unbreakable and love unquenchable and stronger than death, so it suits [the diamond ring] to be worn on the ring finger, the vein of which comes directly from the heart.

In Renaissance literature, diamond-set betrothal rings are mentioned in works by Miguel de Cervantes and Molière. Charles V of France presented Jeanne de Bourbon with a diamond ring on their wedding, as did many other royals and aristocrats during the fourteenth century. Eleanor of Toledo was painted by Agnolo Bronzino soon after her marriage to Cosimo I de' Medici holding her right hand in front of her to display a gold ring with a large diamond. The ring has a Roman intaglio bearing the symbols of love and luck, such as a dove, clasped hands and a cornucopia.

The enduring hardness of the jewel and its resistance to fire and blows of the hammer made it the perfect symbol of the fidelity promised in marriage vows, and once it was discovered in the late fifteenth century that diamond powder could 'polish' another hard diamond and unlock its sparkle, things really began to take off. By the sixteenth century no royal marriage was complete unless it was sealed by a diamond ring.

In an album of miniatures documenting the marriage ceremony of Italian nobles Costanzo Sforza and Camilla D'Aragona in 1475, currently housed within the Vatican Library, the symbolism on the diamond is seen in all its glory. Hymen, the god of marriage, is pictured crowned with roses, wearing a tunic patterned with flames and diamond rings standing in front of an altar on which two burning torches are united by another large diamond ring. The accompanying verse states:

Two torches in one ring of burning fire
Two wills, two hearts, two passions
Are bonded in marriage by a diamond

Two years later, Mary, Duchess of Burgundy was given a diamond ring on her betrothal to the holy Roman Emperor Maximilian of Austria. Diamonds in various shapes were fashioned to form her initial, 'M', with crowns on the ring's shoulders (i.e. the section of the ring that leads up to and supports the head where the stone sits), signifying her royal status. From that time onwards the diamond became the ultimate seal of agreement for promises made at the wedding ceremony.

In the late 1700s, when the French Emperor Napoleon Bonaparte proposed to his beloved Joséphine de Beauharnais with a ring, it featured two pear-cut stones touching each other in the centre: a blue sapphire and a white diamond. Engraved on the inside of the ring were the words '*toi et moi toujours*', and ever since, these rings have been known as 'you and me' rings.

The connection between the strength of diamonds and the enduring promise of a marriage contract has appealed since the inception of diamond rings – as did the fact that diamonds sparkle like no other gemstone. But as we know, a ring – no matter how eye-catchingly beautiful – can't ensure a successful outcome. Even in 1798, the *Lady's Monthly Museum* magazine acknowledged that the ring could only serve as a reminder of one's commitment, recommending its readers to 'always wear your wedding ring for therein lies more virtue than is usually imagined – if you are ruffled unawares, assaulted with improper thoughts or tempted in any way against your duty cast your eye upon it and call to mind who gave it to you, where it was received and what passed at that solemn time.' If this advice was adhered to in modern times, plenty of divorce lawyers might be out of business. Of course, rings don't bind people who don't want to stay together, and yet, nonetheless, diamonds are credited with a sense of permanence, which, combined with their indomitable strength, makes them a favourite stone to represent commitment.

As we know, the diamond was connected to the nuptial arena as far back as the medieval period and yet many theorize that it was South African diamond jewellers De Beers and their catchy 1947 advertising slogan, 'A Diamond is Forever' that was responsible for the dominance of the diamond in the marriage market. Whilst they may not have come up with the concept, following the South African diamond discoveries of 1867, more stones were available than ever before, and suddenly everyone could get their hands on one. Diamonds were democratized, displayed in every jeweller's catalogue, offering designs fashioned from clusters of diamonds. Tiffany's devised a new setting in 1886, raising the stone above six claws, so light could shine from all sides of the gem, effectively announcing an engagement to the world before a word was spoken.

Even in the twenty-first century, when people tend to marry later, after they've formed forthright views about style and have probably already bought a fair bit of jewellery for themselves, the practice of presenting an engagement ring endures. It states with archaic simplicity: I've laid claim to this person. The ring remains a manifestation of the relationship, acting as a physical signifier of the couple's intentions to honour the contract of marriage they are due to sign. Often the ring is regarded as a family heirloom to be passed down through generations, so classic styles have generally prevailed. Having said that, these days anything goes for an engagement ring, from affordable semi-precious stones to platinum skulls. Anyone who chooses a diamond, therefore, has done so because they desire one. Perhaps they are an old-fashioned romantic believing that true love forever is encapsulated in the stone. Plus, the value of a diamond never dims, and contemporary designers make them relevant for younger generations to wear in exciting new ways. Gen Z have embraced lab-grown diamonds, created to be chemically identical in an oven, believing they make an 'ethical' choice. But that's yet to be proven,* and there is certainly no future store of value in the stone, but maybe that doesn't matter. We live in the age of recycling now – whether that's diamonds, rings or, indeed, partners.

FEDE RINGS

'*Fede*' rings emerged during the Middle Ages and remained popular for the next 600 years. They featured the motif of two clasped hands joined at the bezel (the grooved frame holding a gemstone in place), representing the joining of hands of the couple at a marriage ceremony, a practice that dates back to ancient Rome known as *dextrarum iunctio*, whereby the joining of hands, not the exchange of rings, consecrated a marriage. One broad gold hoop in the British Museum features two clasped hands at the end of a foliated band with an inscription running underneath that reads: 'Ile ever bee/constant to thee'. The clasped hands were described as 'handfast', signifying an attachment usually leading to marriage.

---

* The claims that lab-grown diamonds have a low carbon footprint have yet to be proven. It depends on the energy, chemical, material, water and waste management of the factory where they are produced. The manufacturing process is energy-intensive, requiring temperatures similar to 20 per cent that of the sun's surface. Over 60 per cent of lab-grown diamonds are mass-produced in China and India, where the majority of grid electricity is generated from coal. In response to the climate crisis, a few laboratories are using direct air capture to extract CO_2 from the air before it's synthesized and placed into clean energy-powered chemical reactors where a diamond will grow. Boucheron, one of Paris's oldest jewellery *maisons*, are setting fine jewels with a NASA-grade material called Aerogel, previously used to capture stardust and insulate the Mars rover unit. Time will tell if these new technologies capture the imagination of the AI generation in the same way old-style stones from the earth have for thousands of years.

During the eighteenth century, the *fede* featured insignias such as padlocks and flaming torches, representative of constancy and passion. *Fedes* were also given to celebrate the bonds of friendship. The charm of these rings at the time was that whilst they spoke of admiration, they didn't commit the donor to anything binding. Rather, they were a message of devotion or a love letter to somebody. A similar design is found in Ireland. The Claddagh ring features a single bezel of two clasped hands holding a heart, to demonstrate the pledging of trust and friendship. There is a school of thought that holds that, during the late eighteenth century, a Galway goldsmith called Richard Joyce added a crown above the heart, indicating the loyalty between two people. People began to use his version of the ring as wedding bands and slowly the design took the name of the small fishing village where Joyce lived: Claddagh. Now it's called the 'hearts and hands' ring and is passed down through families as well as worn in contemporary ceremonies.

When the Irish potato famine devastated the country from 1845 onwards, propelling as many as 2.5 million people to leave Ireland, many emigrating to the United States, they took their Claddagh rings with them. Wearing a Claddagh ring would have connected these migrants to their home, reminding them of their Irish customs and heritage as they acclimatized themselves to life in another country. They would also have functioned as a badge of identification, just as much as a sprig of shamrock in a buttonhole, to make them easily recognizable to others of Irish blood. It was reported by the *New York Times* that after the 9/11 terror attacks on the World Trade Center, 200 Claddagh rings were found in the rubble of the Twin Towers. The new generation have embraced the Claddagh and even use it to send a coded message: worn with the crown facing down to the knuckle means the wearer is still single; the crown reversed signals 'taken'.

WEDDING RING

We might think of wedding rings today as plain bands worn, in part, to anchor the more valuable engagement ring. Traditionally, however, betrothed couples would gift each other a gimmel hoop to wear during the engagement. Gimmel rings take their names from the Latin *gemellus*, meaning 'twin', as the ring was formed by two interlocking hoops. Sometimes these rings were reunited at the wedding ceremony to form a complete ring on the bride's finger, signifying the joining of two lives. The reunited ring confirmed that each party gave their consent to proceed with the marriage, and the hoops were inscribed with the names of the couple and often a quotation from the Bible to remind them of the indissolubility of a marriage. Canon law prevailed, and for this, all that was required was the mutual consent of both parties. In addition to uttering words, there were certain signs and symbols that could indicate consent. The holding of hands and the giving of a ring were two of these visible signs.

No one knows exactly why three interlocking rings in yellow, white and rose gold are called Russian wedding rings, but some believe they symbolize the Christian belief in the Father, Son and Holy Ghost coming together to form the Holy Trinity. Traditionally, the rings are blessed during the wedding ceremony and exchanged between the couple three times. During the 1920s, the French jeweller Louis Cartier was inspired by these rings and asked his friend Jean Cocteau, the avant-garde designer, to create a ring using three entwined hoops in different-coloured gold – and so three-hoop rings came back into fashion. The resulting Trinity ring sits on the edge of jewellery and sculpture and has been worn by Grace Kelly and King Charles III of England, amongst other luminaries. Its success endures not only due to its impeccable design, but also the powerful personal symbolism held between the hoops. Non-religious couples view the hoops as connectors of the past, present and future of their relationship, and they can also represent sentimental attachments to certain cycles of life – marriages, births and anniversaries. At the end of the day, its power lies in the fact that it bears witness to your life.

Historically in Jewish wedding ceremonies, the rings were weightier, taking the form of pieces of architecture. They were significant in the wedding as they consecrate the central act of the ceremony, as the groom, placing the ring on the bride's finger, pronounces, 'Behold, thou art consecrated unto me with this ring according to the law of Moses and Israel.' Although elaborate in form they never contained gemstones, which was a proscription dating back to the Middle Ages, although some are embellished with colourful enamel and engraved with the Hebrew words *mazel tov* (good luck). Three hundred of these rings are known, which are mostly housed in museum collections. Strangely, their use in Jewish ceremonies is neither documented in Jewish sources of literature or law, nor in pictorial form. However, a Christian scholar, J. J. Schudt, commenting on Jewish ceremonies in 1714 that he'd witnessed in Frankfurt, wrote that when the ring was placed on the bride's finger it was 'usually engraved with the words "good luck"'. The striking miniature buildings on the ring are thought by some to represent the Temple of Jerusalem. Others thought they might depict the home in which the couple would live and create their family life together. Indeed, the golden metal ring holds aloft a small architectural gem constructed in the manner of a miniature house, complete with decorative details of Gothic windows and gabled roofs supported by columns at the corners, often with enamelled flowers blossoming outside. But unromantic scholars dismiss this idea, insisting they represent public buildings such as Solomon's Temple or the Dome of the Rock. Some offer Hebrew inscriptions such as 'I am my beloved's, and my beloved is mine'.

Poesy rings

In the Middle Ages, at a time when love, passion and gallantry were idealized and celebrated, loving sentiments were inscribed on the outside of rings in French, which was regarded as the universal language of love. Recently, a late medieval gold ring was discovered by a metal detectorist engraved with the French translation of 'I desire to serve you'. Chivalric objects such as these made a popular gift in the fifteenth century, emblematic of the fashionable courtly love tradition. Anyone who could afford a gold ring such as this would have been amongst the elite who could understand French. Poesy (or 'motto') rings expressed love between couples and friends. These mottoes were little poems typically translated as romanticisms such as 'Wear this for me' or 'My heart belongs to you', and the words were interspersed with enamelled leaves, pansies or roses around the letters in decorative scripts. The flowers and plants appearing alongside the script acted as metaphors for feelings and tender emotions. The oak leaf symbolized loyalty and strength, and pansies referenced the French *pensée*, or 'think of me'. Cupid with his bow and arrow depicted love, whilst some feature a stag eating dittany – a medicinal herb believed to cure wounds, including those caused by Cupid's arrow.

In due course, the messages became private, concealed inside the loop, only able to be read by the receiver of the ring. Often, they expressed strong emotions and were sent as tokens of desire. Unlike betrothal rings, however, whilst saying quite a lot, the ring didn't commit the giver to anything binding. In William Shakespeare's *The Merchant of Venice*, Nerissa is angry with Gratiano when she discovers he has discarded the ring she had given him inscribed with 'Love me and leave me not'.

> What talk you of the posy or the value?
> You swore to me, when I did give it you,
> That you would wear it till your hour of death,
> And that it should lie with you within your
> grave . . .

Longer messages such as '*restez comme vous êtes*' – 'stay as you are' – were spelt out in enamel. In time, jewellers carried an inventory of rings with popular stock phrases so buyers could choose feelings off-the-shelf, as it were.

In a way, poesies were forerunners of the fashion for acrostic jewels. This tradition began in 1806, with the French jeweller Mellerio dits Meller – founded in 1613, who counted Marie de' Medici and Marie Antoinette as clients – who made jewels imbued with secret messages coded in precious stones. Each gemstone represented its first letter. Thus, the word 'adore' was denoted by amethyst, diamond, opal, ruby and emerald. Others might be phonetic puns. One diamond and mother-of-pearl ring made in 1800 is inscribed with the letters LACD, which in French sounds like '*elle a cédé*' – a triumphant message that proclaims 'she has yielded'. Emperor Napoleon was an inveterate letter writer, and from the early days of his love with Joséphine right up to their bitter divorce, they kept in touch through intimate letters. As well as conveying his thoughts and feelings through his writing, he also sent his beloved sparkling gemstones, commissioned from Chaumet, in which special names, dates and affectionate messages were expressed. Another romantic sovereign, King Edward VIII, gave his paramour Wallis Simpson a grand emerald version of a poesy ring in 1936, the year her divorce from Ernest Simpson was granted, in which the words 'We are ours now' were inscribed on the inside.

Sentimental dates and messages are still inscribed in rings, albeit using less florid language and script. These days inscriptions are likely to bear reference to the *au courant* trend of self-love, with modern mantras such as *dream* or *believe* picked out in a broad array of gemstones by contemporary designers. There's no secret code to unpick there, because most people wouldn't know the names of these lesser-known gems, but I've seen codes spelt out on rings using diamond dots and dashes – definitely a secret message until the day you come across a Morse code translator.

Mourning rings

The concept of memento mori, Latin for 'remember death', is the ancient practice of reflecting on our mortality that dates back to the Greek philosopher Socrates. Symbolic tropes reminding one of death appeared in funerary art, architecture and macabre rings from the Medieval period, which were worn as a decorative missive reminding one of the fleetingness of life. Objects reminiscent of death were worn by the living as a protection against the temptations of this world in order to ensure acceptance in the next. Mortality had always been a theme in jewels, but by the eighteenth century this imagery merged with the emotional experience of mourning, making them more personal and allegorical in their design. Rings might be enamelled in black and engraved with the initials of the deceased and their coat of arms, possibly with a funerary urn, or broken columns of Roman ruins beside a stream to represent eternity. These would be given out to the departed's friends, family and servants according to wishes in their will. When Lord Nelson was killed at Trafalgar, his family arranged for fifty-four rings to be distributed in his memory. The rings were decorated with Nelson's initials, heraldic achievements and motto – *Palmam qui Meruit Ferat* – and inscribed with the words: 'Lost to his country 21 Octr 1805 Aged 47'. Mourning rings were worn to serve as a reminder of the individual and as a celebration of vanished love. Rather than the vibrant colour palette used to express the promise of love, these rings were created in sombre shades of black jet, onyx, dark tortoise and bog oak as tangible reminders of death, occasionally lightened with a shimmering pearl.

Plaited or braided hair, believed to contain the essence

of the dead, woven into ciphers and secreted in glass compartments within the mourning ring, allowed the wearer to hold their loved one in their hand and close to their heart. Other times the hair would be incorporated in the design, perhaps dropping from a weeping willow tree bordered by pearls, which were representative of teardrops. Hair had to be cut from the living, otherwise it would be too brittle to weave and braid, so some would leave locks of their hair with solicitors to be used in their memorial jewellery after their death. Queen Victoria lodged her hair, Prince Albert's and that of her children with the Crown jeweller to guarantee its authenticity. Hair was also a reminder of death's presence woven into the texture of life and something carried with you.

Whilst our modern sense might find this custom macabre, the modern equivalent of cremation rings, made from the ashes of the deceased person, would have likely astonished the Victorians. First the carbon is extracted from at least 500gm of ashes or 5gm of hair, then, using special presses, this is made into graphite and finally a diamond, which shines with an entire new life. Whilst perhaps not to the Victorians' taste, it would have no doubt appealed to the Egyptians and their belief in immortality, resurrection and rebirth, and I for one think they would have liked to see their dead sparkling their way into many different afterlives.

The woman who ushered in the fashion for mourning jewels was Queen Victoria, following the early death of her beloved husband Prince Albert in 1861. Colour was removed from her dress for the remainder of her life and she favoured mourning jewels or pale pearls and diamonds. The entire country was plunged into mourning with her and the ledgers of Garrard, the Crown jeweller at the time, reflect the flurry amongst the court for suitable mourning jewellery. Lockets displaying miniatures of Prince Albert, stick pins and inky-black Whitby jet carved with crosses, clouds, cherubs and heart motifs on mourning rings were produced in volume for the Queen to distribute as remembrances. Some were engraved on the reverse with the sombre words: 'In remembrance of the beloved Prince, Dec. 14th, 1861, from VR'.

Eventually Queen Victoria took herself out of her self-imposed exile from public life and resumed travelling abroad. Many years later, Harold Nicolson recorded in a letter to his wife, Vita Sackville-West, a story that had been repeated to him by George Peel, who, as a young man in 1888, went to Florence for the unveiling of the renovated Duomo. Whilst George waited, he watched from the crowd as a carriage drew up just in front with Queen Victoria and her lady-in-waiting inside. He noticed that the Queen fumbled in her corsage and took out a locket, which she held up to the cathedral at the moment of unveiling. Later, he asked the lady-in-waiting what it meant. 'Oh, it was a miniature of the Prince Consort,' she told him. 'She always holds it up so that he can see something beautiful or interesting.'

Nowadays, we can look back at vivid images and recordings of loved ones, or we might carry their image with us on our mobile phone. At that time, however, many believed a hair was the one thing that acted as a tangible keepsake of a life. Maybe it imparted a sense that you might meet again; material proof that they exist somewhere else, perhaps. A mourning ring gives a person a physical connection with their lost loved one and, when embellished with meaningful motifs, can also act as a social commentary of their life together. When Queen Victoria died, Henry Bell, the Crown jeweller at Garrard, was summoned to Osborne House on the Isle of Wight to sort out her large jewellery collection. Amongst the jewels in purple leather cases embossed with the Queen's cipher were twenty-four memorial rings. Over her long reign, Queen Victoria suffered several losses, including that of her daughter Alice, who died aged thirty-five. Recently, an enamel cross centring on an onyx heart with the name 'Alice' inscribed beneath a coronet, holding a lock of her hair, was auctioned at Sotheby's.

SNAKE RINGS

Queen Victoria also set a fashion for serpent rings in motion when Prince Albert presented her with an emerald and diamond engagement ring of a snake with ruby eyes. A coiled snake biting its tail is called an *ouroboros* – 'tail-devourer' in Greek – and represents an eternal circle. The gemstones would have also reinforced the message of eternal love, since rubies represent passion and diamonds are forever.

The Victorians' love of sentimentality meant many snake rings were set with turquoise, the colour of the forget-me-not, so wearing a serpent that is a symbol of eternity, coupled with the turquoise, sent the plea 'don't forget to love me'. Variations included two snakes intertwined, one made from yellow gold and the other from diamonds, with a miniature version of a padlock declaring the wearer was a captive of love.

Queen Victoria may have renewed interest in the snake, but it is actually one of the oldest symbols in the world. Ancient Egyptians believed that the first living creature to came out of primeval earth was the serpent, and as such it represented the beginning of life. A snake's ability to shed its skin also made it a symbol of death, rebirth, transformation and immortality. Throughout Christian history, however, the serpent has been associated with the devil, sin and temptation. Since the Old Testament Bible story in the Book of Genesis, where the serpent appears in the Garden of Eden and convinces Eve to eat the forbidden fruit from the tree of knowledge, snakes symbolically signal evil or danger. The snake can physically shed its own skin, but never its deadly symbolism.

The serpent has appeared in every culture, civilization and religion, carrying with it rich yet ambiguous symbolism. These intriguing creatures evoke fear and venom but are also associated with wisdom and healing. Jewellers have long been fascinated with the snake's serpentine line in sinuous forms wrapped around fingers, its shape providing a technical challenge and decorative possibilities, as well as with interpreting the many facets of its meaning. In statues from Imperial Rome, women are depicted wearing up to five gold serpent bracelets and rings, high on the arm and coiled around fingers and wrists. Recent archaeological excavations have also revealed a great number of golden snake jewels.

The snake was fully embraced as a motif in the art nouveau period at the end of the nineteenth century, and by the 1960s, a whole new form of snake with a seductive allure redolent of the Cleopatra syndrome emerged at Bulgari. In 1962, when actress Elizabeth Taylor was filming *Cleopatra* in Rome, she was photographed wearing a gold-and-diamond Serpenti bracelet, comprising a coiled gold band with the head of the snake concealing the dial of a tiny, pear-shaped watch. From that moment, the image of the snake rose to new heights of desirability, in tune with the new female attitude in the 1960s whereby women were no longer afraid to flaunt their allure and wear a symbol often associated with sin and seduction. By 1968, Diana Vreeland, the legendary fashion editor of *Vogue*, wrote in a memo to her staff, 'Don't forget the serpent . . . it should be on every finger and all wrists; the serpent is the motif of the hour in jewellery. We cannot see enough of them'.

POISON RINGS

The death of the great Carthaginian soldier Hannibal in 183 BCE didn't come by the venomous poison of a snake bite, but through swallowing a fatal toxin hidden inside a small ring. From then on, rings with cavities inside have been described as 'poison rings'. Ever since antiquity, rings had been an easy way to transport and administer a lethal mixture of tasteless and odourless arsenic: adversaries could be dispatched with a flick of a ring cover, whilst the poison was slipped into what the suspect believed was a convivial glass of wine.

Death by poison reached its peak in Renaissance Italy. Toxic substances were prepared by physicians and alchemists to be deployed by wealthy families to remove human obstacles in their quest for power. At that time, it wasn't possible to detect poisoning, which added to the uncertainty, suspicion and frequent accusations of this method of killing. It was an era characterized by intrigue, violence and assassination. Murder in political circles was so frequent that when a prominent person died, poisoning was always mooted as the cause. During this period of history nobody believed in the natural death of royalty, popes or cardinals. Foul poison play was always suggested as a possible cause.

Catherine de' Medici, Queen of France, is thought to have used a poison ring on a number of her enemies. Yet although one prominent Medici, Ippolito, was known to have died of poisoning, historians generally concur that the Medicis' role in popular history as the dark masters of killing by poison is exaggerated. The other most eminent family of the Renaissance, the Borgias, had a fearsome reputation as poisoners, which was strengthened by the belief that they never travelled without cantarella powders, an arsenical compound which was said to be capable of inducing instantaneous as well as delayed death. Although the Borgias had little knowledge of chemistry, the efficiency of their poison was said to have been tested on animals or slaves, and it was claimed that the Borgias fortified their poisons by feeding arsenic to toads in order to use the urine, though experts think this might well be anecdotal. Nonetheless, it would have been a useful story to spread as a veiled threat to political opponents.

The European age of enlightenment was the era of the goldsmiths, who were reaching new levels of craftsmanship and design. The goldsmith's bench was considered the best training ground for all artists in whatever sphere they wished to work, as Donatello, Sandro Botticelli and Benvenuto Cellini can attest. A new virtuosity in jewellery design was apparent, flaunted by young noblemen who were often painted wearing their jewels. Amongst these were exquisitely crafted poison rings decorated in arabesque motifs, with floral designs and extravagant enamelling using highly sophisticated techniques. At the time, jewellery and religion were powerfully intwined, so instead of their real, nefarious purposes, they could appear as innocent containers for relics, bone, ash or a piece of crucifix wood.

The frequent talk of poisoning at this time incited many people to carry an antidote with them, and recipes were duly published for anti-poison oils. Of course, you'd also need a container to hold this liquid, and so anti-poison rings began to be commissioned. The mysticism and power of rock crystal was believed to guard against poison, so this appeared in rings, goblets and chalices as protection. One Italian silver ring on display at London's V&A Museum features an onyx intaglio of a scorpion to evoke the zodiac sign. The scorpion was associated with water and believed to produce a cooling effect, which, when used on a ring, acted as a sign of protection against deadly substances.

By the sixteenth century, poison rings were wildly popular and could also conveniently be used to end the life of the wearer. Giuseppe Verdi used a poison ring as a vehicle for Lady Leonora to die by suicide in the opera *Il trovatore*, and the Marquis de Condorcet took poison from his ring in 1794 to avoid the guillotine. Arsenic remained the poison of choice because it was easy to come by and undetectable – that was, until a test was developed to measure poison in tissue and body fluids in 1836.

Poison rings are still popular with contemporary jewellery designers, though they are created with less insidious intentions. Nowadays they are more likely to be used as a 'pill box' for tablets with health-giving benefits as opposed to deadly ones. Some people like their jewels to have moving parts, so they can play with them like toys, and the poison ring fulfils that role with the added benefit of being a secret treasure trove, with a tiny space to carry something small and personal at the wearer's fingertips. Poison rings have emerged from the dark side with a playful role on fingers, rather than a deadly one. Nonetheless, the concept remains clandestine, for it is designed for no one else to know – a cloak-and-dagger affair between you and your jeweller.

VINAIGRETTE RING

During the nineteenth century, rings were made with cavities to contain more agreeable fluids. Vinaigrette rings performed much the same function as a pomander chasing away bad odours and could be flipped open by a richly decorated button and a pleasing smell would be released throughout the day. Perfumes were made from aromatic herbs and spices such as sage, cinnamon, lavender, mint and rosemary mixed with alcohol, and they protected the wearer from foul smells, but also the deadly waft of cholera from coming too close. Also, when the sponge inside was only soaked in vinegar, it could prevent the wearer from fainting.

Some vinaigrette rings were hung on chains. The Royal Collection is home to a gold and enamel vinaigrette with a domed lid over the basin container, enamelled with sprays of flowers on a chain of enamel links ending in an enamelled marquise-shaped finger ring. The long chains swung from side to side in a flirtatious manner and the ring accessory took the place of the fans used during the summer months to attract attention and relay secret messages to potential suitors.

Should the summer pollen bring on a sneeze, another functional ring came to a woman's rescue. As it was described by *The Young Ladies' Journal* in 1870, 'This pretty invention consists of two rings, one round for the little finger which is connected by a gold chain with an octagonal ring, bearing the name of the owner, through which the handkerchief is passed'. The handkerchief must have been small and thin to fit through a relatively tiny hoop and yet the challenge for the designer was to transform an object of function into a pretty jewel. The ring had far more important offices than allowing a lady to dab her nose, in any case. In those days, the only acceptable way for a woman to communicate her feelings and intentions in public was through non-verbal communication, so, whilst she might bat her eyelashes or offer a sideways glance, the handkerchief ring proved to be a much more efficient messenger of coded signals. For example, when the handkerchief was removed from its ring and folded, it meant, 'I want to speak with you', whilst 'I love you' was conveyed by brushing it softly against her cheek. Winding the handkerchief around the forefinger broke the disappointing news to a suitor that a lady was engaged. In flirtations, these rings made for invaluable instruments for lovers.

PORTRAIT RINGS

The portrait ring made a solid declaration of love between a couple. Wealthy families also commissioned designs of loved ones, and sovereigns gave them to subjects to reward loyalty, friendship and trusted service. Poignantly, on her deathbed, it was found that Queen Elizabeth I's locket ring had a secret compartment believed to contain a portrait of her mother, Anne Boleyn. The dynastic importance of royal marriages was affirmed by the gifts of rings that contained portraits of the happy couple to those who attended the ceremony. In the case of Archduchess Marie-Antoinette to Louis XVI, miniature portrait rings were given to the maids of honour.

Mostly these portraits were painted using watercolours and a tiny brush on ivory or vellum, whilst others used enamel on metal. They were set onto a ring, as well as other types of jewellery, and preserved under a piece of glass or rock crystal, or, in some more lavish cases, a flat portrait diamond. These thin, flat jewels were minimally faceted along their perimeters, giving them a glass-like quality used to enhance the portrait.

Russia made this type of jewel her own. Each generation of tsars was associated with diamond portraits, especially to mark their coronations. Catherine the Great gave many miniatures as badges of office embellished by a single diamond cover. The largest portrait diamond known, the historic 25-carat Tafelstein, covers the miniature of Alexander I, portrayed full-length standing in military uniform painted on ivory which was cut to the same shape as the transparent stone. The four daughters of Nicholas II and Alexandra were represented as a group of miniatures, each covered by a portrait diamond and framed by old-cut brilliants. These portraits dating from 1906 could also be hung from a chain at the neck and were believed to have belonged to a favourite aunt, the Grand Duchess Olga. But another diamond set featuring portraits of all the children was owned by the Empress and taken with her on her final journey to imprisonment at Ekaterinburg, where it would have been taken from her following the executions in 1918 and sold by the Bolsheviks.

Whilst often the motivation was love, some portrait miniatures were created for a political purpose. Queen Henrietta Maria gave portrait rings of Charles I, who was dressed in a lace collar and garter sash, crowned with rose diamonds, in the years leading up to the Civil War to those who supported the Royalist cause. Following his execution, when aristocrats had to be more circumspect about their political affiliations, many 'loyal' courtiers began to conceal their portrait rings underneath plain covers. Leaders were painted in heroic style for rings following success on the battlefield or negotiating table. Emperor Napoleon, Lord Horatio Nelson and the Duke of Wellington all featured on portrait rings, emulating the noble style set by royalty.

Even staunch republicans succumbed to the practice. The American statesman and national hero Benjamin Franklin's portrait was painted in miniature on ivory and enamel, housed underneath glass and set in a ring. His role as drafter and signatory on the United States Declaration of Independence fascinated British potter Josiah Wedgwood, who created a series of ceramic portraits of the diplomat. In 1799, Franklin wrote to his daughter, 'A variety of [clay medallions] have been made of different sizes, some to be set in the lids of snuffboxes, and some so small as to be worn in rings, and the numbers sold are incredible. These, with the pictures, busts and prints ... have made your father's face as well-known as that of the moon.'

The high point of the art was during the Georgian period, and these 'portraits in little', as they were called, shine a light on the behaviour and visual culture of the time. This was a period of great social and economic change as the Industrial Revolution cranked up, and new canals, railways and roads meant people were on the move. Women were also literally moving with greater ease, as clothing became lighter and easier to wear compared with the long trains and hoops that had restricted movement. High society was obsessed with socializing every night during the season; there were balls, dances and costume galas and, during the day, new pleasure gardens opened to allow people to promenade, satisfying the Georgian's infatuation with seeing and being seen.

The act of looking and watching was important to late eighteenth-century society. In spite of this intense socializing, social codes limited public interaction between members of the opposite sex, so looks could more easily be exchanged than words. Small miniature rings were exchanged as emotionally charged jewels with meaning and a way to remember a loved one at all times by keeping their portable portrait on a finger.

By the end of the century, having only one eye painted and placed within the ring, rather than a full face portrait, became highly fashionable. Some believe this practice was begun by King George IV, who included a painting of his eye in a love letter to the twice-widowed Maria Fitzherbert, with whom he exchanged at least eleven jewelled 'his and hers' portraits throughout their relationship and morganatic marriage. Richard Cosway was the official miniature painter to the King, able to capture the powerful symbol of the eye – described as the mirror to the soul – in a way that reflected someone's innermost thoughts and feelings. These became fashionable because they were a form of elegant intimacy, making the subject tangible for the wearer, yet anonymous to onlookers. Some piercing gazes were no larger than a fingernail and were bordered with pearls or diamonds. The emotional sentiment was obvious when a tiny *trompe l'oeil* tear was visible, painted to exemplify the pain experienced upon parting.

By the end of the nineteenth century, photography struck a death blow to the miniature ring and in a blink of an eye, the tradition died out. Flirting between couples through this medium was over. Of course, for today's swipe-right generation, having a portrait painted would be much too lengthy a process.

Cocktail rings

The exuberantly large cocktail ring, mostly set with a colourful semi-precious stone, is what we might describe now as a 'knuckleduster'. This statement piece of jewellery encapsulates the jazz age, a term coined by writer F. Scott Fitzgerald to describe the decadence of the Prohibition era, when the US instigated a nationwide constitutional ban on the production, importation, transportation and sale of alcohol from 1920 to 1933. It was a time of glamorous flappers, dashing bootleggers, secret speakeasies and hedonistic excess, when 'cocktails' (served in teacups to disguise the drinking of liquor), were all the rage – said to have been created to make the contraband alcohol more palatable.

Cocktail rings were about Martinis, fast automobiles and the freedom for women to flaunt their independence. Bejewelled hands drew attention to their newfound liberties of smoking, drinking and applying bright red lipstick in public. There was a sense of exuberance and generosity in the glossy metallic folds of a cocktail ring, which could also feature large paste stones, not only precious jewels. This was a fashion for all women who were finding the energy and confidence of the time as intoxicating as cocktails themselves.

When Prohibition was repealed and the gold standard for the US dollar was waived, a surge of optimism was ignited, and clients were eager for showy, bold jewels. By the mid-1930s, the entirely new American style called 'cocktail' was entrenched in people's imaginations. It ricocheted around the world and was even adopted by the fine Parisian jewellers' *maisons*. Women's style was evolving fast: the new lines of tailored skirts and padded shoulders emphasized feminine strength as many women had taken on the roles of men away at war, and large rings highlighted their newfound power. Platinum, diamonds and gold were in short supply, so jewellers concentrated on large semi-precious stones such as citrine and aquamarine to achieve the requisite impact.

And these rings never really went away. One solitary cocktail ring still makes a stylish statement about strength for any woman. During the 1990s, they became known as 'right hand rings' and were pushed towards career women, bachelorettes, divorcees and widows – anyone who wasn't or didn't wish to be married. 'You can have a showy ring if you live independently' was the thinking behind it. The days of women waiting to be given a ring were over; women were buying jewellery for themselves. In effect, they were setting their own style agenda for designers to follow. Cocktail rings were about self-expression, a jewel of frivolity for hard-working professionals earning their own money, a showy display that told the world they had charge of their own lives. This phenomenon was only further stoked by creative women designing for other women.

New female designers such as Victoire de Castellane at Dior began to shake up the world of fine jewellery with an unconventional attitude to what 'precious' should look like. She made rings of shocking sumptuousness using materials and motifs that appeared almost like costume jewellery. With brilliant imaginings and a coquettish wit, she made a visceral connection between precious gemstones and a modern desire for jewels that reflected how women lived. Everything had a new and fresh exuberance, from the size and bright colour of unusual gemstones to the glittery, fluorescent enamel. Then, in response to the #MeToo movement that started in 2006, designers began creating what I call 'armour' rings, worn by the likes of the Olsen twins, Rihanna and Miley Cyrus. They were on the large cocktail size, spreading from the knuckle rising halfway up the finger and fierce-looking, like something a medieval knight might have worn on his finger for protection. These rings echoed another phase in women's stories, encapsulating an era as well as a fashion.

CHAPTER THREE

BEADS

Easily taken for granted and consigned to children's toys, it is impossible to talk about the history of the world told through jewellery without paying due reverence to the humble bead. Ancient, universal and primal, these small, perforated discs have witnessed the evolution of human behaviour in all its positivity and ugliness and have the power to reveal key stories about our past.

In certain parts of the world, beads – fashioned out of everything from plant seeds and fish vertebrae to grooved teeth and ostrich egg shells – are amongst the most common objects found in prehistoric excavations. When beads originated around 100,000 years ago, they had great significance to the wearer as well as the wider community. Their primary role was at this time protective, and stones and pebbles with naturally occurring holes through the centre, called hag stones in the British Isles and Northern Europe, were believed to possess shielding qualities. Even today there are people who look for hag stones along a shoreline to take home and string into a pebble-bead necklace to ward off bad luck and misfortune. During the Victorian era they were strung outside stables as anti-witch devices to protect a horse from being 'hagridden'. Animals found to be exhausted in the morning were believed by superstitious stablemen to have been stolen and ridden by witches or hags during the night; the idea that the cramped and unhealthy conditions of the stables could be to blame didn't, at the time, cross their minds. Recently, I've seen contemporary necklaces made from what look like massive grey hag stones created by young designers from cardboard tubes. I don't think they'd scare a witch away, but they answer the modern need to keep unsustainability at bay.

During the Upper Palaeolithic period, one adult Magdalenian female was buried adorned with seventy deer-teeth beads featuring an engraved design smeared with red ochre. Although, on the whole, objects buried with an individual are chosen by someone else rather than the deceased, they still deliver messages that speak to us through the centuries. Objects may have been chosen based on what it was believed the dead would need in the afterlife or to convey a statement to those attending the person's funeral. The placement and positioning of the deer-teeth beads in this case reveal aspects of early socializing and belief structures, and indicates she may have been a leader, since it was important to the community who buried her that the beads were secured prominently on her body.

Beads also provided our first social network. As empires fell and people migrated, crafting methods and materials dispersed; indeed, new analysis of seashell beads discovered by archaeologists suggests that humans have been making beaded fashion statements for at least 150,000 years. It is possible beads had been used to barter and trade for supplies; thus, beads provide a glimpse into the history of global trade. We know the only source of lapis lazuli for the ancient Egyptians was in north-eastern Afghanistan, so it must have been imported, as must obsidian, from Anatolian Turkey. An obsidian necklace was found in northern Iraq, with cowrie shells filled with red ochre, which must have come from the sea, so the necklace contained elements that originated many hundreds of miles apart. The demand for brightly coloured beads was probably a significant factor in the development of these early trade networks.

Glass 'trade' beads have been found in the US, Canada and throughout Latin America. A handful of blue beads discovered in an ancient Alaskan settlement at Punyik Point are believed to be the first European items found in America. The plant fibres holding the beads meant archaeologists could use accelerator mass spectrometry carbon dating to find out when the plants were alive. 'We almost fell over backwards. It came back saying [the plant was alive at] some time during the 1400s,' said the University of Alaska's study co-author, Mike Kunz. 'This was the earliest that indubitably European materials show up in the New World by overland transport.' Having travelled along the Silk Road, they would have made the journey across the Bering Strait, from the Pacific to the Arctic Ocean, in a kayak. Indigenous North Americans, therefore, were trading beads decades before the arrival of Columbus in the Bahamas in 1492.

Stretching back 70,000 years ago, the marine shell *Nassarius kraussianus* was used in a clutch of pea-sized perforated beads discovered inside South Africa's Blombos Cave. The South African archaeologist Professor Christopher Henshilwood stated on their discovery in 2004 that they are probably amongst the first examples of abstract thought seen in our ancestors. 'The beads carry a symbolic message. Symbolism is the basis for all that comes afterwards including cave art, personal ornaments and other sophisticated behaviours,' he said. 'Even in today's world, where you're talking about computers – it's about storing information outside of the human brain. The evidence from Blombos Cave is that humans were using symbolism 75,000 years ago.' In other words, the beads demonstrate organized modern behaviour.

EGYPTIAN STONES

Believe it or not, we have the Egyptians to thank for the concept of fakes. By the fifth millennium BCE in ancient Egypt, natural pebbles and bone had been supplemented for beads of finely worked carnelian, lapis lazuli, jasper, feldspar and turquoise. The colour light-blue, with its associations with fertility and the sky, was rare and therefore highly prized in ancient Egypt.

Due to this shortage, the Egyptians produced faience, created from quartz, alkaline salts, lime and mineral-based colourants, to make shiny imitation stones. In fact, this brightly coloured glaze was a forerunner of glass. Despite the fact they were man-made, faience beads were thought to be filled with the undying shimmer of the sun and imbued, therefore, with magical powers of rebirth.

From sophisticated gold-capped carnelian beads and amethyst bead scarabs to simply strung clay beads, the materials varied according to the status of the wearer. King Tutankhamun, for example, wore a *menat* necklace, which was composed of rows of beads made out of a mix of lapis lazuli, turquoise, carnelian, faience and agate on a bronze and copper alloy with a long pendant and decorated fastening which hung down behind the shoulder. These necklaces were reserved exclusively for divinity, so worn by pharaohs only. King Senwosret II's hieroglyphic pectoral, featuring inlays of turquoise suspended from a necklace including turquoise ball beads and green feldspar drops, tells a tale of life at the time. It was found amongst the jewellery in the tomb of Princess Sithathoriunet, and the gold, carnelian, lapis lazuli, green feldspar and garnet pendant necklace with the composition of falcons and the sun as symbols of protection and eternal life signified her royal status. The power and protection of the beads were siphoned off for the King's benefit alone, however, which is why his name, rather than that of the princess, appears on her jewellery.

Ancient Egyptian style became highly sought after in the wake of these archaeological excavations. When Egyptologists Howard Carter and Lord Carnarvon unearthed the treasures in Tutankhamun's tomb in 1922, a fashion for Egyptomania swept through Paris, London and New York. This is why the bead became a popular jazz age jewel. Long art deco sautoirs featured gemstone beads often ending with a beaded tassel or oversized geometric pendant, which was also detachable for use as a brooch; you could say it was a kind of jazz age pectoral. Once again, the Egyptians' favourite colour scheme of turquoise, lapis lazuli and carnelian was back in vogue, and design motifs included Egyptian representations of lotus blossoms, scarabs and the Eye of Horus. In the same way the Egyptians used faience, the art deco beaded style had its own copyist material. In 1909, Belgian chemist Leo Baekeland created the first synthetic plastic, named 'Bakelite', which became fashionable during the 1920s. The beauty of the new material was that it could be shaped, faceted, moulded and drilled to make highly polished beads. Bakelite beads made an attractive and affordable replacement for precious stones in many colours, including marbled and translucent shades with striking patterns, mimicking the fashion for scarab and lotus flower designs.

At the other end of the spectrum, Cartier began sourcing genuine Egyptian treasures from Eastern bazaars to feature on their beaded necklaces. Ancient sacred rams in bright blue faience and beads dating from 900 BCE were bordered by diamonds and onyx in the Cartier workshop, maintaining the purity of the ancient style whilst also updating it for a modern audience. Magnificent bib necklaces were created with glistening bubbles of ruby, sapphire and emerald beads, replacing the fashion for simple diamond rivières. The world was changing fast in favour of an art deco modernity that was glamorous and optimistic about a future filled with innovations in transport, machines and feats of human engineering. It's interesting that this advance forward required looking back to the past and that ancient Egyptian-style beads were chosen to reflect the streamlined spirit of the era. Sometimes the oldest things can appear the most modern.

WAMPUM BEADS

Native North Americans used beadwork to express themselves artistically in a tradition that was also compatible with a nomadic lifestyle. Beads are one of the smallest portable objects, so they could be easily packed up and transported. In the absence of both the written word and an understanding of different languages, beaded adornment became an important element of Native American messaging.

Their favoured wampum beads were made from seashells. White beads came from the whelk, a sea snail with a spiral shape, and purple ones were harvested in the summer from the quahog clam. The meat was consumed, and the shell was broken into small blocks with a reed drill or stone, creating a hole. Then they were ground into tubular shapes by rolling or rubbing against a stone and strung with sinew or plant fibre. It was delicate and skilful work, and the colour of the beads conveyed meaning. For the Algonquian people, white beads represented purity, light and brightness, whilst purple beads signified war, grief and death. Both colours together denoted the duality of the world: light and dark; woman and man; sun and moon.

Wampum was the Native Americans' go-to for every occasion: births, marriages, death, the signing of treaties, remembrance storytelling and political diplomacy. Every message was spoken through belts or strings of beads or woven into symbolic and mnemonic patterns. Words spoken during an agreement were made into wampum to be used at ceremonies. Beads took the form of visual memory keepers, and so wampum became objects of historical record. For example, the 1,000-year-old Hiawatha wampum belt symbolizes the agreement between six warring Iroquois nations to support each other. The great white pine, the tree of peace, appears in the centre with the six nations depicted as squares around the edges, a white line connecting all of the symbols for each tribe, which denotes the unity of the Iroquois.

The Iroquois tribes continued to use wampum to convey important messages during turbulent times, such as the French and Indian War in 1754–1763, when a white beaded belt brought by messenger meant the sender spoke words of peace, whereas a string of dark purple heralded words of war. If the receivers agreed with the message, they kept the belt; if not, the belt was cut up. It wasn't until the arrival of Europeans in the North American continent 500 years ago that wampum adopted a monetary value to trade with indigenous tribes. Eventually, the introduction of European metal tools revolutionized the production of wampum. Dutch colonists discovered the importance of the beads as a means of exchange between tribes and began mass-producing them in workshops. But by then the Native Americans were hooked on the new exotic European glass beads – more on which shortly.

CARNELIAN BEADS

The notion of jewels as portable wealth is deeply rooted. For centuries traders risked their lives transporting beads, goods and spices across 4,000 miles of unsafe and tough terrain, such as the Gobi Desert and Pamir Mountains. For 1,500 years, the Silk Road – a complex and spidery network of paths – connected civilizations in the East and West. This began during China's Han dynasty, when nomadic tribes traversed vast plains stretching across Central Asia, carrying gifts of silk for the Emperor to maintain peaceful relations.

This route – named in the nineteenth century by German geologist Ferdinand von Richthofen – played a significant role in connecting the arts between East and West. Jewellery cultures travelled with the beads, which were traded as decorative objects and used as a form of currency to barter. And it wasn't goods alone that reached new territories; people, religions and ideas voyaged between diverse cultures, and this exchange of information was crucial for multicultural cities to develop new craft techniques, styles and designs. The importance of different cultural contributions to jewels and beadwork was recognized recently when London's V&A Museum appointed their first curator of jewellery to lead on the acquisition, documentation, presentation and interpretation of their jewellery collection with a distinct focus on diaspora.

Despite all the challenges such a journey would have presented, one unassuming ninth-century carnelian bead somehow made its way safely along the Silk Road from Gujarat in India to Derbyshire in the UK, where it was discovered in 1982. It was buried amongst 264 bodies in a mass grave – the first Viking camp found outside Scandinavia – resting near the skull of one particularly large warrior. Initially considered an unremarkable trinket, it languished in a Tupperware box for years until it was noticed by Dr Cat Jarman, a bio-archaeologist specializing in the Viking age. She was intrigued. How had it travelled the remarkable distance from India to deepest, darkest Derbyshire? Carnelian wasn't a stone natural to Britain, so she wanted to piece together its journey and the strong global connections that had made it possible. This prompted the discovery that the Vikings had hitched onto the established silk roads by venturing to Russia and using a network of river routes via the Dnieper River to the Black Sea, along the Volga to the Caspian Sea and on to Constantinople and the bazaars of Baghdad, the capital of the Abbasid dynasty of caliphs. The small yet mighty carnelian beads were proof of the link between these disparate worlds.

Small objects can unravel more than just their journey. Even in the distant past, there were fashions to follow. The chic of the exotic played a part in Viking style; wearing something decorative, like a carnelian bead, set you apart, denoted status and connections, and was viewed as a luxury item. There is evidence that Viking women wore beads decoratively, whereas the men had them in small pouches around their waist, suggesting they used them for trading. Through a combination of isotope and trace element analysis to match chemical signatures in specific beads to possible sources from a geographic region, Dr Jarman could trace the bead's life and prove that women had held more powerful roles in society than previously believed. It had been assumed females stayed at home and didn't take part in Viking raiding parties abroad, but there was a high percentage of females found in the Derbyshire grave who weren't local Anglo-Saxon women, but who had migrated from Scandinavia. A few of the skeletons were sword-bearing warrior women, whereas others were merchant traders buried with their weights and scales.

There are still artisanal carnelian mines in Gujarat today producing similar beads, where sixth-generation bead makers use the same ancient techniques to file, sand and drill beads, as the skill and knowledge are passed on with each generation. This Viking bead therefore appeared contemporary, like a semi-precious stone knick-knack you can pick up in any store. Dr Jarman couldn't pinpoint the exact mine in Gujarat where the bead might have been cut, but she's hopeful that this information might be garnered from the bead itself in the future.

GLASS BEADS

Glass was introduced to Britain by the Romans in lumps or tesserae, which were small cubes often originally intended for mosaics and sometimes pillaged from Roman ruins. Small pieces of glass were melted and moulded inside a heated furnace or over the hot coals of a fire and then wound on a thin metal rod called a mandrel, which also drilled the hole.

The only real difference in the method of melting glass in modern times is that we use a torch instead of a furnace and mandrels are made of steel instead of iron – but otherwise the practice is largely unchanged. Then as now, shapes were formed by rolling the bead on a smooth block whilst the glass was still soft. The beads were left plain or decorated with blobs or trails of a different-coloured glass.

In part, the Vikings left their homelands to discover new trading networks to establish a future income. Furs, amber, beads, silks and ivory made valuable commodities alongside the active acquisition of human chattel, which was a key part of their economy. This was one of the primary objectives of Viking raids and military campaigns, and the result was a massive increase in the numbers of enslaved people in Scandinavia. Surviving locals from their raids would be herded into slave pens and set to work. They were made up of British, Irish, Slav, who gave their name to the word slave, or any other peoples they encountered. The Vikings needed people to work in the burgeoning towns they were helping to create on their voyages, and foreign slaves were put to work building their enormous fleets of ships. It was a profitable operation. The slaves were taken to the markets in Constantinople and Baghdad, feeding the need in the Constantinople culture for slaves, who were a part of the society, particularly in harems and armies. The history of the bead has borne witness to human trafficking.

When the Roman Empire conquered Egypt, they had learnt the craft of glass-making as the process of making faience basically led to the discovery of a glass glaze. The Egyptians were the first to use glass in their culture, and the Romans simply improved on their production methods. By the end of the first century CE there was large-scale manufacturing of glass, making it a commonly available material in the Roman world. Rome's emergence as the dominant political, military and economic power in the Mediterranean was a major factor in attracting skilled craftsmen to set up workshops in the city. The establishment of the Roman industry coincided with the invention of glass-blowing, which revolutionized ancient glass production.

Glass-blowing developed in the Syro-Palestinian region in the early first century BCE and is thought to have come to Rome with craftsmen and slaves after the area's annexation to the Roman world. This new technique enabled larger quantities of beads to be made in a range of shapes relatively quickly and inexpensively. A myriad of sizes and colours of glass beads were traded as far east as China and Korea as well as north to Scandinavia and south to Ethiopia and India. These coloured glass beads in certain cases were made to imitate semi-precious stones like carnelian, amethyst, emerald, sapphire and garnet.

Following the fall of the Roman Empire, glass-making declined until the twelfth century, when the success of the Venetian Republic gave rise to the revival of various arts and crafts, including the production of glass. Since glass factories often caught fire, the practice became confined by law in 1291 to the island of Murano, where the tradition remains to this day. The removal of glass-makers from the city also had the benefit of enabling Venice to keep their methods of producing glass secret. One of these secret methods was the revival of the mille-fiori technique, whereby artisans used canes of glass to create patterns resembling a thousand flowers. They were named retrospectively in *The Curiosities of Glass Making*, published in 1849. Prior to that, millefiori were described as mosaic beads. At the time, the rosetta or chevron bead was created by using the millefiori tech-nique, which involved fusing together a multitude of hollow glass canes into patterns of stars or flowers. They were taken by seamen, such as Christopher Columbus, as gifts to secure passage through dangerous waters. By 1606, there were 251 bead-making firms recorded in Murano alone, and Venetian glassmakers are thought to have made some 100,000 varieties of bead types and designs for global export.

Although the majority of Venetian glassmakers named in historical documents were men (the work was considered too rigorous for women), some female glassmakers did exist during the sixteenth century, and they formed their own guild. The Venetian Republic acknowledged the artistic talents of glass masters who introduced innovative methods, but only one woman – Marietta Barovier – was given permission to lead her own furnace in the sixteenth century. Later, when Venice fell to Napoleon in 1797, many of the city's glassmakers were taken to France to reveal their production methods, and thus new bead production centres grew in Holland and the Czech Republic. The Bohemian beads were cut on water-powered cutting wheels. The world-famous Daniel Swarovski was born into a glass-cutting family in northern Bohemia in 1833 and when he visited the 'First Electricity Exhibition' in Vienna, he determined to improve the cutting and faceting (the polishing process) of glass beads and patented the first electric glass-cutting machine. His name has signified quality glass beads ever since.

MANHATTAN BEADS

European colonization of America had disastrous effects on indigenous Native American peoples and their societies. As we know, Native Americans had been making their wampum, buffalo bone and stone beads long before the Europeans arrived, but the new glass beads became a popular novelty and in time replaced these natural materials. The loss of land was a major factor. Where once the Sioux, the Kiowa and Comanches lived alongside buffalo herds, taking from them meat for food, skins for tents and bones for bead-making and tools, white settlers took over their reservations and brought cattle with them, which competed for land with the wild buffalo. Buffalo became an even more finite resource once German leather makers created technology that allowed their hides to be tanned more efficiently and economically. Within decades, the buffalo went from numbering tens of millions to within a hair's breadth of extinction. Slaughtering the great herds was a way to starve and devastate the Native North American tribes, and their economy, livelihood and culture has never fully recovered.

Colonizers and settlers took advantage of the Native Americans in a series of deals and treaties. The alleged Dutch purchase of the island of Manhattan in 1625 for a handful of beads worth a total of $24 has gone down in history as one of the biggest swindles ever perpetrated. The transaction has become part of New York's origin story, even if some historians insist that it has no factual basis. In any case, historians concur that there were cultural differences in the understanding of property rights and ownership and exactly what the meaning of 'selling' land meant. It's unlikely that the Native Americans would have irrevocably sold their ancestral land. The exchange between the Lenape Indians and Peter Minuit, Director of the New Netherland colony, doesn't itself seem to be in question, instead it's the meaning of the exchange that is queried. The Lenape were probably under the impression that they were selling the right to live on the island, or use its resources, as they themselves did, not the right to own the land forever, much less the right to prevent other people from using it. It's most likely to have been a disastrous case of communication failure. Indigenous peoples understood land as being a shared space, and it wasn't common for land to be sold permanently, which is what the Dutch would have understood as ownership.

To our modern sensibilities, a few beads sounds like a meagre payment for a large area of land. The oft repeated idea that they sold their ancestral land for trinkets implies they were unsophisticated and oblivious to the value of what they had. And yet, writes Aja Raden in *Stoned*, 'Value is relative'. She points out that the swampy land of Manhattan wasn't coveted at the time and the Dutchman's beaded jewels were rare and exotic, so the Native Americans might have been satisfied with the price they were paid.

SLAVE BEADS

By the sixteenth century, European glass beads were introduced to East Africa by Portuguese and Dutch traders to be exchanged for the most valuable resources of the region: gold, copper, tobacco, ivory, rhinoceros horn, tortoiseshell – and human beings. It didn't take long for the trade in beads to become established and gradually glass beads replaced existing bead currencies made with local materials such as shell. Glass beads were relatively cheap to produce, hugely variable in terms of design and relatively easy to ship over land and sea, satisfying the demand and popularity.

Occasionally trade beads are still found on the tidal foreshore of London's River Thames, possibly dropped as a ship was loading cargo for a trip to Africa. A glass chevron bead resides in the British Museum which may have been to Africa, the Americas and back, unsold and returned to Bristol. It represents the 'triangular' trade network of goods between India, Europe and Africa. In response to the demand for what became known as 'African slave beads', manufacturers scaled up the production of these beads. Glass beads accounted for 7 per cent of total Venetian glass exports in the sixteenth century and by the late eighteenth century that figure was over 70 per cent.

The dark side of beads associated with the slave trade casts a long shadow. Did the craftspeople in Murano moulding glass over the heat of an oil lamp know the destination and nefarious use of their creations? We can't know. In any event, they would have been too busy providing for their families. At this time the most common job for women in Venice was stringing glass beads. These *impira-ressa* would thread several kilos of beads from Murano onto long needles which contained a cotton string inside. The threads of beads would be tied together in a bunch with a set number of strings, like a unit of measurement, so that merchants and explorers using the beads for trade knew how many beads they were carrying. The hours were long and badly paid, but a day's work would provide the family with a loaf of bread. *Impiraressa* were some of the first women to go on strike in Italy, demanding greater rights and respect, but this was in 1904, when demand for these bunches of beads was essentially over. Their work was recognized 100 years later when the Art of Glass Beads was awarded Intangible Cultural Heritage status.

If the glassmakers themselves didn't know, the Venetian Republic certainly did. Officials were only too keen to foster their most successful export. In mid-1700, Sir James Wright, His Majesty's Minister in Venice, commented on the trading necessity of glass beads: 'It seems our African Trade always suffers whenever we are not regularly supply'd with Beads: it is very certain that the indolence of the Venetians together with the number of their feast days prevent them from supplying us with the necessary quantity.'

It's hard to believe something so small and pretty could lie at the heart of this shameful history, yet beads are artifacts of an inhumane system of power and exploitation. And yet we need to understand the reality. We can't know the exact story of an individual bead, but they provide a moment of hands-on history. It's important they are kept and their tale told so we don't forget and history doesn't repeat itself. When Edward Enninful, whose family roots are in Ghana, became editor-in-chief of *British Vogue*, I remember at one of our first meetings, whilst discussing a proposed jewellery shoot, he said, 'Never put a chain on a black model.' The painful connotations of slavery persist.

Because glass is durable, it can provide clues about who lived in an area and when, signalling the presence of enslaved individuals whose lives we wouldn't otherwise know about. Smithsonian bead expert Laurie Burgess helped date a plantation site in Virginia using excavated beads, which showed that the site existed in the 1720s–1760s, which is valuable because these people were often left out of the historical record.

Human behaviour may not change – human trafficking sadly continues to this day – and yet the role of the bead in the evil practice has ended.

Prayer beads

From ancient to modern times, beads have been employed to assist the faithful in prayer. The practice of counting prayers using a string of beads is ancient; there are legends of St Anthony in the third century counting his prayers with pebbles. Most cultures have used beads as a form of art and prayer, and it's likely that Christians, Hindus and Muslims borrowed the idea from each other – possibly as the culture was carried along the Silk Road with the beads. So entwined are beads and prayers that the word bead derives from the Old English word *ebed*, meaning 'prayer' or 'request'. Many religious people use prayer beads every day as mnemonic aids to count their prayers. In the case of rosaries, knots and beads appear at regular intervals along a cord or chain, each one connoting a prayer and instilling a specific prayer rhythm for worship. In Lindisfarne, off the Northumberland coast of Britain, a ninth-century rosary made out of salmon vertebrae has been discovered.

In Buddhism, mala beads are used to count the recitations of prayers and devotional invocations or mantras, a process that allows the practitioner to accumulate merit; the more recitations, the more merit accrued. This strand has a standard 108 beads, an auspicious number rooted in early Buddhist literature and pre-Buddhist Indian belief. In Islamic practice, there are ninety-nine beads to facilitate the recitation of the ninety-nine names of God, with the pendant bead commonly used as the chief spacer and handle, which the person praying can use to keep track of a circuit. The Greek Orthodox rosary kombologion can have any number of beads, which would have originally been woollen knots tied into the string, from thirty-three – to symbolize the years Christ spent on earth – to 150.

During Ramadan, the holy month when Muslims fast during daylight hours, worry beads are one way to keep the hands occupied and avoid temptation. They can also help former smokers looking for something to do with idle hands. Now worry beads have morphed from fidget-jewels into power bead bracelets to calm the mind for those wanting spiritual or meditative focus. Countless combinations of semi-precious stones are used in beads for a therapeutic purpose to self-soothe in anxious moments. Worry beads have a new resonance as tactile instruments of comfort to hold onto through worrying times. Each coloured stone aligns with one of the seven chakras, the energy points in the body, for anyone wanting to feel more grounded and balanced. Bead bracelets are combining spiritual journeys and cultural practices. Mala beads are complementing meditation practices for yoga enthusiasts, encouraging them into the present moment.

American designer Jacqueline Rabun reflects on the human experience through her use of gemstones. 'The times that we're living in, they're not very easy times. There's a lot of chaos at the moment, so I think people need to be grounded and supported,' she says. 'It's good to have gemstones around you with their healing qualities.' One of her signature designs is a large organic-shaped polished rutilated quartz bead which you can remove from its gold pendant casing to hold. 'It's calming to hold in the palm of your hand,' she explains. 'The stone and its shape are quite soothing for the soul.' You could call it a modern cross between a rosary and a worry bead to be used in a personal ritual as a reminder of what you want to change and what you want to be. Rabun says it's a discipline, like a beaded form of meditation, to use on a daily basis. In fact, the slow rhythm of stringing and weaving beads can become almost a mediative occupation, helping with relaxation and self-fulfilment. The Egyptians experienced these rhythmic repetitions stringing bead colours and shapes; Native Americans and Africans have also known the benefits of its practice throughout history.

HIPPIE BEADS

By the 1960s, peace was personified by 'hippie' beads. Hippieism was a countercultural movement that rejected the mainstream values of American life at the time. The movement reached its height whilst opposing the American involvement in the Vietnam War and rejection of Cold War diplomacy. Eschewing money, materialism and politics, they preached free love and flower power. Their experimentation, whether in drugs or fashion, was a rejection of conventional wisdom and their parents' generation. The rock musical *Hair* was shocking audiences on Broadway, thrusting counterculture centre stage. It tells the story of a politically active, long-haired group of hippies living a bohemian life in New York City, reflecting the hippie culture and sexual revolution of the 1960s. One scene featured the cast fully naked chanting: 'beads, flowers, freedom and happiness'.

Hippies sought a laid-back way of life, upending conventions and desiring to connect with previous generations. They were fascinated with non-Western cultures, emulating the handmade bead and clothing culture of Africa, India and Native Americans. They adopted kaftans, flared trousers and cheesecloth blouses found in small boutiques smelling of patchouli oil along London's Carnaby Street, and mood rings, dashikis (a colourful, loose-fitting kaftan-style shirt worn in West Africa) and strings of beads became the look.

They also tapped into the Hare Krishna movement, a branch of Hinduism whose name comes from its chant – *Hare Krishna*. It was founded in the sixteenth century by Sri Chaitanya of Bengal, who emphasized the worship of Krishna and believed that chanting the names of God was so powerful that, in addition to one's own meditation on them, they should also be chanted in the streets for the benefit of all. Hare Krishna gained mainstream popularity after the Beatles' George Harrison wrote the ballad 'My Sweet Lord' about the Eastern religions he was studying, repeating part of a Hindu mantra in the lyrics. It remained at the number-one spot in the American music charts for over two months and sparked a multitude of new devotees wearing Tulsi beads in three strands around their necks, who were seen on city street corners and public parks everywhere.

Ever since, beads have signified peace and love. Today, free-spirited teenagers might wear love beads and rosaries in rainbow colours by jewellery designer Diane Kordas but be unaware of their history as they pile them one on top of the other. This is what's called cyclical fashion, each generation looking for their own identity using beads and a little meditative quiet amongst the noise.

EMBROIDERED BEADS

Beads have always been used as a strong non-verbal communicative device, incorporated into many artistic traditions across the globe to express messages. One of these traditions is dress.

The beadwork in costume always tells a story. The Ndebele people in present-day South Africa and Zimbabwe use intricate beadwork as an expression of their cultural identity. Bold geometric designs in beads made a powerful political statement during periods of colonialism and apartheid. When Nelson Mandela wore the costume of a Thembu King, including leopard skin and a beadwork collar, to his trial in 1962, it was part of a wish to delegitimize the authority of a European court in Africa. Now beadwork in South Africa is increasingly associated with a 'traditional' precolonial African identity and an independent past.

Beadwork is still used as a means of marking the different cultural stages of an Ndebele woman's life. A girl's apron is formed from a stiff, folded canvas strip that is tied around the waist, with beads embroidered on the surface, hanging from an upper lace-like bead cloth. Different types of beaded patterns and motifs communicate social and marital status, defining the progression of a woman's life. One example in New York's Metropolitan Museum shows how the dimensionality of the garment encourages the play of light when seen in motion, expressive of a youthful exuberance. Once the woman is married, the aesthetic is different – the beadwork becomes more refined with a subdued colour palette on a background of white beads.

The elaborate beaded dresses that Native American Plains women made – and still make – carry an outward expression of their tribal identity and family values. In the Northern Plains area, the hides most often used for dresses and shirts were mostly made of deer and elk because the skins were thinner, whilst thicker buffalo were mostly used as blankets. Historically, hide dresses were like canvases upon which Plains women expressed their creativity and marked the significant events in their lives. Each Native nation expresses itself in its own unique way, using different colours, symbols, designs and materials. In the way that we might wear a wedding ring to indicate our status in society, beads convey their position and life-altering events. It could be a marriage, the valour of a family member or a particular design meant to honour an individual's accomplishments. The dress connects them to community, family and ancestors, the beaded decorations functioning as symbols and designs conveying a narrative. Both the culture of stitching beads and the family tales they tell are in their blood, so to speak, and passed down through families.

Beaded dresses can also be used in grander occasions that take place within families. The prestige, inheritance and responsibility of figures in authority can be demonstrated as effectively with simple beads as glittering crowns. Whilst not strictly regalia in the manner of the Imperial State Crown dazzling with the oldest gemstones in Christendom, 10,000 crystal beads were hand-stitched onto Queen Elizabeth II's coronation gown in 1953 as indelible links to her new role as monarch. The Queen had made a sovereign observation that her gown should embody the emblems of Great Britain as well as the Dominions of which she would now be Queen.

The embroidery rooms at Norman Hartnell's atelier went into overdrive to interpret these eleven motifs as flowers using silken stitchery, as well as jewelled sequins and beads. The three emblems of the thistle, shamrock and leek to represent Scotland, Ireland and Wales were sewn onto the upper portion of the skirt, to allow more space below for all the combined flowers of the Commonwealth, including the Canadian maple leaf, Australian wattle, New Zealand silver fern, Indian lotus flower and South African protea, all assembled in a floral garland. Each flower or leaf nestled closely around the motherly English Tudor rose, placed in the centre. The embroideries on the wide circle skirt were arranged in three scalloped, graduated tiers bordered with alternating lines of gold bugle beads, diamantés and pearls. The beading took 3,500 hours to complete and once finished, the robe weighed almost seven kilograms. As Deputy Surveyor of the Queen's (now King's) Works of Art, Caroline de Guitaut, says, 'It's probably one of the most important dresses made in the twentieth century – certainly a great piece of British design. The combination of rich fabrics and beautiful embroideries was really Hartnell's absolute signature, and I think the greatest expression of all his career.'

At first Hartnell was reluctant to include the Welsh emblem, preferring to use a graceful daffodil as the national flower. The Garter King of Arms, at the office of the Earl Marshal in Buckingham Palace, opposed him, insistent that the leek was the only correct Welsh emblem. 'The leek I agreed was a most admirable vegetable, full of historic significance and doubtless of health-giving properties, but scarcely noted for its beauty,' argued Hartnell. In the end it was the humble bead that elevated the earthy vegetable into something splendorous to embellish the dress of a queen. Hartnell sprinkled it with the diamond-dew of crystal beads, transforming the leek into a vision of charm amongst the delicate roses and mimosas. As the satin dress glistened on its way down the aisle at Westminster Abbey, it was the beadwork that picked out the emblems that impressed on the world that this young woman was the Queen of the United Kingdom as well as thirty-two sovereign states.

Whilst sheer quantity can be impressive, just one single bead can make just as powerful an impact. Since its inception, the Holocaust History Museum within Yad

Vashem (the World Holocaust Remembrance Center) has displayed articles of clothing that were worn by inmates of concentration camps. I was struck by one grey shirt to which an orange bead was pinned. It belonged to Helen Ryba, who was sent on a march in 1944 to a forced labour camp near Leipzig. She had been a dressmaker, and this single bead reminded her each day that she once had a life – a home, work and a family. The bead embodied the life to which she vowed she would return; as long as the bead was close by, she was able to hold onto a glimmer of hope. The bead gave her strength and determination and, in a certain way, saved her life.

Another single bead sewn into the seam of a jacket tells a similar story of survival. Before the Second World War, there were 120 members in Klara Stern's family – the grandmother of *Game of Thrones* actress Laura Pradelska – but only eight survived the war. When Germany invaded Belgium, Laura's great-uncle Yossele went into hiding in different villages around Antwerp, where he was helped by the resistance network. All the time he kept a diamond bead safely sewn into the seam of his clothes as a talisman of his former life. The diamond had been entrusted to him to make a family ring, which would be presented to Klara to celebrate the birth of her first child. Klara gave birth in a labour camp and her seven-month-old baby boy was taken from her and murdered. She was deported to Auschwitz and liberated in 1945 by the Russian Red Army with nothing but salvaged rags provided by the Red Cross. Yossele found her and delivered the bead. It was the only memento of Klara's past life and she wore it until her death in memory of her slain family. In due course, Laura inherited the bead and wears it set into her engagement ring. 'I'm not a material person,' she explained to me. 'Objects are just things – but what this diamond represents is far more important: resilience, suffering, survival, but most of all, love.'

PLASTIC BEADS

Over time, new technologies have brought advances in bead production, whilst higher efficiency and standards of uniformity have led to mass production. New materials heralded the 'Age of Plastics' and other synthetic polymers seeded the growth of a worldwide industry. Just as glass had replaced beads created with natural stone or shells, in the 1950s glass was being superseded by new plastic beads.

It's hard to imagine now as we battle climate change, but plastics were greeted with huge excitement when they were first created. 'They're brighter, gayer, tougher and often more practical than the material they replace,' wrote Charles A. Breskin in the February edition of *Vogue* in 1943. Pages of colourful polychrome beads were featured on models as *Vogue* alluded to the attraction of plastic beads, which, they urged, weren't created in any way to mimic gemstones, but were covetable in their own right.

Vogue went so far as to declare that it was fine to wear fla-grant fakes, writing: 'They make no effort to supplant real jewels in elegance, and in this very quality lies their chic.'

Breskin and others failed to mention their slow decomposition rate in natural ecosystems, however. Lara Maiklem, author of *Mudlarking*, looks for things of inter-est that have been thrown away, lost or misplaced and washed up along the foreshore of the Thames. She dons a pair of gloves and kneepads and uses her eagle eyes to spot poesy rings, garnet love tokens, Roman coins, medieval pilgrim badges, clay pipes and porcelain lying amongst the mudflats. I asked her what modern equivalents are lost to the river from our society – the objects and daily utensils that unearth the story of how we live. 'We're the plastic age,' she said. 'That's what we're leaving behind. Our ancestors' stuff is all organic so it can go back to where it came from, but our plastic stays floating just under the surface. There are actual islands in the Thames now that are made of wet wipes, so we are changing the geography of the river with our waste, which is quite depressing.'

Plastics began to dominate for their light weight, durability and flexibility, as well as their inexpensive production costs. But the high price being paid by our environment is one that no one calculated. Plastic pol-lution is found in all the world's major waterways and is causing widespread environmental problems. The large-scale production of beads meant they became less valuable, and the arrival of cheap plastics meant beads lost their cache as luxury items. Beads were relegated to something fun and disposable, and in time became divorced from their exoticism and significant history. These are now seasonal items, not objects to be cherished and passed down through a family.

Acrylic reproduction wampum beads are now being mass-produced in China. However, I'm reassured that indigenous artists in the north-eastern United States are still crafting wampum jewellery from the quahog and abalone on a small scale and beadwork remains an integral part of some Native American cultures, especially on the Plains and in western North America. Today, there is a younger generation returning to beadwork and organic materials such as seed beads, shells, quills and feathers in fashion pieces. Elias Jade Not Afraid learnt how to bead whilst growing up in Lodge Grass, Montana, on the Crow Indian Reservation, where he lived in his great-grandmother's old house. 'While living there, I would dig through her large cedar trunk and look at her beadwork,' he says. 'I taught myself how to do the traditional Crow-style beadwork technique.' Designers with Native American backgrounds such as Tania Larsson and Bobby Dues are keeping traditions alive, combining traditional techniques and symbols with innovation and fashion, giving Native Americans a voice on the pages of *Vogue*. Canadian-based Catherine Blackburn, from the Dene tribe, thinks new beading is positive. 'Beadwork showcases the individuality of our histories,' she says. 'Within this space, we can reclaim and celebrate our identities.'

These artists feel there is a certain power in continuing to use materials that were once handled by their ancestors. Carnelian beads, like the one found in the Viking grave, are now in high demand. Young people have become eco-warriors, making sustainability part of their everyday wear. They are returning to the natural beauty of stone beads from the earth as miracles of nature to honour the earth.

Ultimately, a return to stone beads holds within it a hopeful belief in the permanence of the earth. I'm always struck by the simplicity of the lapis lazuli and chrysoprase archaic necklaces fashioned by anthropologist and jewellery designer Pippa Small, striking in their similarity to beads worn by the ancient Egyptians. They are talismans for modern living, but in another life could have been funerary jewellery, like barrel-shaped bead amulets made of carnelian, found at the throat of a mummy, or possibly the asymmetric bead necklace of carnelian, moss agate and quartz found in the Tomb of Wah, a young man who died before he was thirty years old. He must have loved the beaded jewel and worn it often, because it was re-strung for the funeral. The linen cord shows no sign of wear, looking as fresh and desirable as it did thirty-nine centuries earlier.

There's history in every bead. They are connectors through different time periods and civilizations. As humans we happen to have been born at different times and different places but the things we have around us, and the need to adorn ourselves, has always been the same. Ultimately, the tale of the bead is a surprisingly modern one. It speaks of migration, globalization and a shared language allowing us to integrate and understand each other. It's hard not to marvel at the incredible journey of the bead: from the shell of a stationary bivalve, bone or gemstone, which has gone from sacred object to dark commodity to cultural icon, crossing continents and the world, and finally returning to its starting point. Decorating a human body with a power to link us to history whilst remaining relevant for the future, beads are the ultimate recyclable material – combined and recombined through generations, until they form part of our DNA. Each tiny bead allows a vast amount of genetic information to be passed from one generation to the next.

CHAPTER FOUR

CHARMS

As long as there have been humans, there have been superstitions. Jewellery has functioned as tiny protectors against evil ever since *Homo sapiens* roamed the earth. We might think of charms today as the pretty trinkets that adorn bracelets, but across time and spanning cultures worldwide, charms have meant the difference between life and death. From amulets to ward off evils and talismans to attract good luck, charms – be they stones, animal bones or shells – have always been deployed both to repel danger and attract good fortune. It's part of the human condition to want to control what's not in our power, and these tiny objects are the receptacles of our wishful thinking. Millennia later we still hold onto these shields, summon their efficacy in keeping the bad at bay whilst ushering in the positive.

Our ancestors met extraordinary challenges to survive, facing disease, injury and predators every day. A shell, feather or bone worn during a successful hunt might well have been relied on again ... and again. Just for luck. In the same way, we might carry a four-leaf clover or ladybird into exams, job interviews or throughout daily life, in spite of the fact that in the developed world we live in the most peaceful, vaccinated and healthy period in history. Over time, anxieties and fears simply evolve. Our predators exist on social media and now, instead of sabre-tooth tigers, climate change and global warming threaten our existence. Old habits die hard, and whilst our fear responses remain active, we'll always have a place in our life for lucky amulets.

There isn't a culture in the world that doesn't believe in the power of a charm. In Africa it might be a fertility symbol, in the Middle East it might be sacred hands or the hand gestures that are widespread in Italy. In the ancient world, talismans were used for everything from protection against disease to helping in childbirth. Before the nineteenth century, when there was no knowledge of viruses and bacteria, disease and death were accepted as the punitive result of either God's will or supernatural forces.

Hope was pinned not just on devotional rosaries, crosses and votive offerings, but also on ancient magic charms, often made from materials such as red coral or rabbits' feet. Human beings the world over rely on amulets and charms. The form and imagery may vary across cultures and civilizations, but the notion of enhancing protection, luck and good health for the wearer is a universal ritual. In Myanmar owl charms are considered to bring luck, whereas in Ireland that task falls to the shamrock and four-leaf clover. For centuries Scandinavians relied on the symbolism of the Norse god Thor's hammer, a weapon believed to be so powerful it could crush giants and level mountains.

The challenges faced by the human race vary from century to century. The ancient Greeks may have sought protection from snake bites, whereas a modern pressing concern is AI technology. Whatever the fear, the idea that comfort is derived from the ancient practice of wearing a talisman endowed with a helpful meaning persists. Our modern reasons for using charms aren't so very different. Charms are deployed for action in everything from the large and life-threatening ills to the simple wish for calm. Plus, primitive superstitions do survive in our modern life. The centuries-old tradition of protecting yourself with the evil eye is still thriving in many parts of the world. The evil eye is a curse meant to inflict harm, distinct from a cobalt-blue eye charm worn to dispel the curse and ward off the mystic malevolent forces of the world. Our most loved and classic tales concern the battle of good versus evil, so many of us like to imagine we have something magical batting on our side. Charms are at the forefront of this conflict, loaded with mystery and spiritualism. It's a story as old as time itself. Whether or not they help is a matter of conjecture; what mattered then, as it does now, is the wearer's belief that they can. Core conviction is how the talisman proves its magic.

SCARAB BROOCHES

Animals have always been used as mascots for protection. Sometimes the whole animal is deployed, whilst other times just one part of it is used, such as the wishbone, foot or tooth. A scarab beetle might not be the most obvious emblem of good fortune, but the ancient Egyptians imbued the humble dung beetle – the scarab – with magical symbolism, and it's still in use around the world today. There's certainly an unexpected beauty and nobility about the beetle, with its shimmering opalescent emerald-green and blue sheath and diadems of spiky horns upon their heads.

In ancient Egypt, the beetle was associated with the major themes of creation: virility, wisdom, renewal, resurrection and immortality. In fact, the Egyptians believed that this small creature encompassed the meaning of life itself. The action of dung beetles laboriously rolling balls of dung across the earth was likened to the way the sun god rolled the sun across the sky. It is in this way that the beetles became symbols of creation. Plus, the Egyptians noticed that these balls were dropped into holes in the ground, from which later young beetles emerged. From seeing the newly born beetle rise from the dirt, the Egyptians decided the animals had been reborn (when the reality was that the female laid her eggs in the earth and, as they hatched, they turned to the lump of dung as a food source).

The ancient interpretation of this life cycle was that the beetle was immortal, which made it the ideal symbol for people obsessed with the afterlife. Hundreds of thousands of scarab amulets were manufactured in ancient Egypt. Mostly they were small-scale amulets, attached to beads and jewellery and worn by the living to protect them from death – and by the dead to help them on their way into the afterlife. Scarab amulets were placed as rings on the fingers of the deceased, or else wrapped in linen bandages to rest on the heart as a symbol of the resurrection of the body. Ancient Egyptians believed the deceased's heart would be weighed against a feather by the funerary jackal, Anubis, before a panel of forty-two judging divinities. The heart had to be lighter than the feather for the deceased to pass into the next life successfully. When a pharaoh died, his heart was carved out and replaced by a stone rendering of a scarab, since the scarab symbolized transformation and re-birth, as well as protection and luck for their journey to the afterlife.

Ancient Egyptians believed there was inherent virtue in precious stones. Carnelian, turquoise and lapis lazuli, for instance, represented the colour of lifeblood, the fresh green of spring vegetation and the deep blue of water and the sky, respectively. When such a precious stone was engraved with a sacred symbol such as the scarab beetle, it emphasized the combination of special qualities. One of the largest of these scarab beetle talismans resides in the British Museum. At a monumental 1.5m long, carved out of diorite stone and weighing two tons, it is believed to have been made to protect a building. Some smaller existing scarabs are believed to have been gifts exchanged by friends to foster good fortune. Two scarabs in New York's Metropolitan Museum feature inscriptions that read like modern greeting cards: 'May your house flourish every day', whilst the other states: 'May Ra grant you a happy New Year'. How much more chic to send a message via scarab rather than a text.

As I mentioned in Chapter 3, Howard Carter and Lord Carnarvon's discovery in 1922 of Tutankhamun's tomb in the Valley of the Kings sparked what was dubbed 'Egyptomania'. Contemporary designs were inspired by the ancient treasures unearthed in the tomb, including the scarabs. Louis Cartier collected ancient Egyptian antiquities and statuettes and combined them with the strict lines, geometry and unusual colour combinations of the art deco era. Some of his most beautiful jewels were created in the spirit of ancient Egyptian opulence, paying homage to the sphinx, the pharaoh, the obelisk and the scarab, recreating them in carnelian, turquoise and onyx. Cartier scarabs with outstretched wings echoed the majesty of jewels from Tutankhamun's tomb and might well have been unearthed by Carter, such was their beauty. Movie stars and other celebrities soon followed the trend: Mrs Cole Porter wore a belt with a lapis blue scarab set between faience turquoise wings surrounded by sapphires and diamonds on the buckle.

More recently, the mystique of the scarab was revived again when the hundredth anniversary of the discovery of Tutankhamun's tomb was celebrated. Indeed, the scarab makes the perfect symbol for modern audiences and should be honoured as one of nature's indispensable recyclers. In their bid to clear away dirt and droppings, these beetles churn up and aerate the ground, adding fertilizing nitrogen to the soil, making it more suitable for plant life. As such, we should venerate the scarab just as our Egyptian ancestors did. The popularity of Egyptian scarab motifs continuously recurs through history and is constantly reborn for a new generation of trendsetters. The Egyptians were right; the luminous glow of the silver-winged beetle is immortal.

CHARMS FOR CHILDREN

In the ancient Etruscan world, life began with jewellery. Boys as young as nine days old would be covered in magical amulets with a string of bulla pendants across the chest to protect them from illness and bodily harm. Mostly created in sheet gold with a hollow inside, the bulbous-shaped bulla locket was named for the Latin for 'bubbles' and was intended to ward off evil spirits. It's unclear whether girls wore bullae; it's thought they may have worn a lunula, a crescent moon-shaped pendant, for the same purpose. The Romans adopted the custom as children were viewed as vulnerable and in need of protection. Statues testify that they often wore three or more bullae as armbands, or strung on a necklace or bracelet with other pendants. There would be special rituals, blessings and incantations performed over the ornament before it was placed on the child's body; in a way, the bulla was the physical manifestation of the ceremony. Anointing your child with a bulla protected them and also signalled an important message to the wider community that the family had integrated their child into Etruscan social practices and beliefs. Overlaying it with various spells meant the bulla was useful in different areas of life; they could be used as love charms, talismans to help warriors on their campaigns or as protection from disease.

The elite wore gold bullae, but less expensive versions were made of leather, bronze, wood or amber, depending on the economic and social status of the family. Amber, the fossilized resin of pine trees, had a special resonance, because when the translucent honey-coloured substance is rubbed, it can produce what feels like an electric charge. Indeed, the word 'electricity' is derived from the Greek word for amber: *electrum*. In time, the Romans adopted the practice of wearing both bullae and amber. The Romans lived in fear of supernatural powers and forces they did not understand, believing that children were particularly vulnerable. The Roman author Pliny wrote in *Naturalis Historia*, 2,000 years ago, that: 'a collar of amber beads worn about the neck of young infants is a single preservative to them against secret poison and a counter-charm for witchcraft and sorcery'.

It seems strange to us now, but the model of an erect phallus made in amber was regarded by the Romans as the most powerful protection against dark forces and evil spirits. Such charms featured winged, penis-headed animals, and Romans wore them openly and soldiers clung on to them before going into battle. Most curious of all to our modern sensibilities, however, is that this sexual image adorned children. The truth about charms is that the symbol doesn't contain the significance; its real power lies in the protection it characterizes, and hopefully, embodies. When faced with the high mortality rates in babies and infants, few of whom reached the age of ten years old, no self-respecting Roman parent would neglect to source a bulla or amber charm for their child. The amber phallus was a hopeful cure-all, designed to protect a child from every kind of ailment and bad luck.

DEVOTIONAL CHARMS

The Romans crucified Jesus in Judea in CE 30 on a cross, so perhaps it follows that crosses are worn around necks as a form of spiritual protection dating back to that period. However, the cross was worn as an amulet thousands of years before Christ was crucified. Crosses crafted out of soapstone with a loophole for hanging as a pendant were around in ancient Cyprus between 4000 and 2500 BCE, and it's thought the symbol originally derived from representations in cruciform figures of women giving birth, arms outstretched.

The ancient Egyptian ankh symbol for life is a relative of the Christian cross, although it also predates that image by centuries. The ankh is viewed as a magic key of knowledge, with the loops at the top deemed to be a sign of eternity. Gods and goddesses were portrayed holding ankhs and it was one of the ancient Egyptians' most popular amulets which, like the scarab, was a funerary charm for a prosperous afterlife. It's not known if these crosses survived to influence early Christians; it wasn't until years later that the cross symbol was taken up as the Christian representation of the life and death of Jesus Christ.

Most people who follow a religious creed trust in sacred amulets that symbolize their faith, calling on the assistance of the god or gods they recognize to face the trials of life. Jews wear a Star of David, whilst many Sikhs feel unprotected from temptation and evil without a metal bangle, called the Kara, on their wrist. The use of amulets is widespread in Buddhism in the form of a cross-legged Pha, a laughing Buddha, which is thought to bring luck. These amulets often feature words from the religions' holy books. In Islam, it is forbidden to carry a pictorial image of Allah, so the most potent charm is the written word. It could be a gold pendant inscribed with a verse from the Qur'an or as simple as a bead with the word Allah on one side and Muhammad on the reverse.

Devotional amulets are created in most materials, from silver and gold to rock crystal and wood. During the Renaissance period, when it was thought beautiful objects were somehow closer to God, jewellers tried to outdo each other in terms of intricate details and embellishments on the crucifix pendants and miniature cross-shaped reliquaries they produced. Possibly, the patrons who commissioned extravagant crosses felt it was money well spent, guaranteeing an exclusive entrance to the kingdom of heaven. Although simpler versions were worn by the truly devout, ostentatious crosses became charged magical artefacts, believed by some to protect the wearer, prove their devotion and even promise a miracle or two. Or so they hoped.

Until the last fifty years or so, these crucifixes were broadly worn by people with a firm faith. However, since the Western world has become increasingly secular, the cross survives as a 'spiritual' sign. The image of a cross on a chain being held up to repel sources of danger has been ingrained in our imaginations in horror films as the ultimate amulet in the battle of good versus evil. The widespread use of Christian crosses and Islamic crescent moons could be deemed cultural appropriation – but in a way they are as much cultural symbols as religious and worn in that light they can become signifiers of all faiths, and none. Devotional symbols increasingly, I like to think, can be pillars of co-existence and peace. At the end of the day, devotional amulets are symbols of hope to live a better life – even for those who may not be religious.

Whilst the ancient Egyptians relied on scarabs for a safe passage along the treacherous road to the afterlife, travellers for centuries have sought sanctuary from pieces of turquoise, known as the traveller's stone, as well as the religious symbol of St Christopher. Millions of people around the world don't set off on a journey without the reassurance of their St Christopher medallion attached to a chain on their body or in a car, believing that looking on the image of the martyred saint means they won't die that day. On other days when not on the move, St Christopher might not receive such attentive devotion. So little is known about St Christopher's life that in 1969 his feast day was removed from the Church's calendar, but this hasn't dented his popularity – proof that we like to hold onto something comforting, especially when far away from home or managing the unnatural sensation of travelling 35,000 feet above the earth. The actress Marlene Dietrich suffered from a fear of flying, so travelled with a St Christopher charm boosted by a lucky rabbit's foot, Star of David and a cross. Can't be too careful, I suppose.

Coral charms

Coral has long been believed to have great amuletic power. It is considered by many Christians to be symbolic of Christ's blood, as the vibrant red of the coral twigs are reminiscent of red blood vessels. During the Renaissance period, coral branches were mounted in silver as christening gifts and it became common practice for coral amulets to be placed around a baby's neck. Coral was prized as a thing of beauty, rarity and exoticism but also as a multi-purpose protector. Women liked to wear coral bracelets and necklaces to guard them against the evil eye and as a symbol of wisdom and happiness. In his painting *The Three Graces*, the Italian artist Raphael depicts young beauties holding apples from the garden of Hesperides; they are nude except for dazzling red coral necklaces.

Coral is a complex marine organism and has a calciferous skeleton which is sometimes dark orange or blood red. It isn't extracted from the earth like other stones – it grows on the seabed – so it is often referred to as the 'tree of life of the ocean'. Sailors and fishermen felt carrying a piece of coral would protect them from the hazards of the sea; indeed, some Italian fishermen to this day won't set out without a coral charm. A particular deep-red coral was first discovered in the Strait of Sicily between

Pantelleria and Sciacca, when three trawler captains on a fishing trip found what they termed 'red gold' in their nets. The news spread fast and soon there was a 'coral rush', with a large number of boats pouring into the area. By the 1880s there were nearly 100 factories in the southwestern coast of Sicily, around the town of Sciacca, dedicated to processing coral, prompting the *New York Times* to report in 1881 that 'nearly the whole of the vast yield of the Mediterranean is brought to this town'. By strange irony, the most widespread symbolic values of coral over the centuries is its apotropaic and healing qualities, when coral reefs are endangered and badly need healing themselves. Pollution, overharvesting and climate change have led to many reefs being declared endangered, and more than 180 countries restrict the export of red coral harvested after 1969.

Sciacca coral is now repurposed into a range of figures and lucky motifs important to the superstitious in Italy. Small red *cornicelli* flourish in the city of Naples, like talismanic chilli pepper trinkets. When these new peppers arrived from South America, they became favourites in the kitchen hung as charms because they looked so much like red coral horn amulets created in the spirit of the bull for strength. Horn signs appeared in wall paintings on Etruscan tombs as indicators that great horned animals were symbolic of power and courage. In Italian folklore, coral is used to counter the *malocchio* (the evil eye), sly, jealous glances or envious comments, as it was believed that even a quick look could deliver harm. The curved shapes of a chilli were made in smooth coral in a way that looks like a cross between a chilli and a horn, so they absorb the power of both their 'parents'.

Horns are extended into another charm. The *mano cornuto* (*mano* means hand, *corno*, horn) began as a fleeting pre-Roman gesture with two fingers pointing downwards. The idea was to make the hand appear like an animal's horned head about to charge and, flashed at anything sinister or threatening, would spirit it away. The gesture graduated to small amulets worn for personal defence. Like the peppers, these are sold widely around Europe, fashioned out of everything from gold to plastic.

There was a curious tradition in the Mediterranean during the nineteenth century that touching the hump of a hunchback was lucky and a harbinger of well-being. Soon *scartellati* (a Neapolitan hunchback) were fashioned in coral and gold and taken home as good-luck charms and mementoes by tourists. They are portrayed as figurative charms for pendants and necklaces by Dolce & Gabbana as a well-dressed man wearing a coat and top hat. Assertively Italian in their aesthetic, the designers who share their countrymen's superstitious natures believe in liberally piling on symbols of abundance – just for luck. These *scartellati* have delightful gem-studded horseshoes and emerald four-leaf clovers twinkling in their hand, whilst he makes the *mano cornuto* with the other. Who hasn't suffered from the *malocchio* at some point? Young girls complain about the idea of the frenemy – a friend who doesn't actually wish you well – all the time. No wonder hand gestures in coral still carry powerful messages.

The Penca de Balangandan

The Penca de Balangandan is an Afro-Brazilian amulet with a mixture of metal charms and baubles hanging from a central fastener on a chain. 'Balangandan' is an onomatopoeic word meant to evoke the sounds of the clustered charms as they knock and jostle against each other. When not in use they hung around a door tinkling in the breeze like a dreamcatcher. These charms date back to the eighteenth century. In Portuguese, *penca* means a bouquet or bunch, and this brooch-like silver arc has two globe fasteners at either end, which open to allow more charms to be added along the chain. They frequently depicted plants and fruits from Brazil, like cocoa pods, gourds and pomegranates split open revealing their seeds for fertility, along with parrots and crosses. Sometimes a gourd vessel was included, which represented the female womb in some African cultures, or the Mediterranean 'fig' gesture of a thumb protruding from between the curled index and middle fingers. This hand gesture is believed to divert the evil eye and is the feminine version of the Roman phallus; as the fig makes a comment about female sexuality, the hand indicates the presence of female genitalia. The idea is that when the charm is flashed, it preoccupies the evil spirit, which is immediately distracted from its malevolent purpose.

Essentially, the Penca de Balangandan is a twinkling mishmash of cultural motifs and symbols composed to reflect the life of the wearer, some chosen to impart good fortune, prosperity, good health or gratitude for surviving a misfortune like an accident or illness. They were originally worn by slave women of African descent as amulets around wrists and on thick chain belts hung around the waist as more tinkling charms were added and the silver weight increased. Like a modern charm bracelet, each balangandan was unique and reflected the life path of its wearer. I like to imagine the diverse life of one Bahian woman whose balangandan, now housed in the British Museum, boasts the following charms: a Brazilian coin dated 1860; three keys; a melon; two fish; a sea turtle locket; a heart with a fist; a dove; an anchor; a dice; a pomegranate; a guava; an axe; a chimney sweep; bagpipes; a human figure with a moon on its head; and a sphere with a star on each side. The balangandan was meant to bring good luck by calling on the symbolism attached to the various items – and I hope it did for her.

Rather than wait your whole life to amass such a hoard of charms, silver Penca de Balangandan bracelets are now available with a ready-made range of charms for good fortune, fertility, happiness and prosperity with a mix of evil eyes, a Carmen Miranda, water buffalo, lucky cat, hut with a palm tree, coffee bean, parrot and sailing ship. Sometimes they include a fig sign, which has outlived its magical or sexual origins and is now sold as a simple charm all over the world, to people with no notion that their jaunty-looking amulet has been symbolic since ancient times of female genitals. Now, it's more generally understood to be a signal of defiance – as in: 'I don't give a fig'.

CHATELAINE CHARMS

One reason for women to jangle with chains of trinkets was that before they carried bags, they needed a way to keep useful accessories on their person. At most in the nineteenth century, women carried 'reticules': tiny fabric pouches with barely enough space for a handkerchief. The concept of waist-hung containers is universal across all cultures; the Japanese carried *netsuke* and the Chinese had small, embroidered purses. In the Western world, women secured their collections of trinkets and keys onto a chain attached to the waist of their dress. These were called 'chatelaine' and carried items such as button hooks, mirrors, needlework tools, scent bottles and small pencils – basically anything deemed necessary for the daily upkeep of the household.

Chatelaine evolved to include charms and amulets, and style soon began to trump usefulness. The chatelaine contained all the elements for the house, but the choice of charms, love lockets and amulets provided an opportunity for the wearer to show her personality. They were intensely personal and, as such, a forerunner of the modern charm bracelet. Small metal notebooks added to chatelaines had holders on the side for the original pencil and the notebook would open accordion-style, revealing ten small images, pictures and photographs. These women didn't have iPhones to pull out and show off photos – instead, loved ones were firmly attached to their waists. Women even started announcing their arrival in a room by the clanking of their chatelaines, and all the major jewellery houses, such as Tiffany, Boucheron and Lalique, made them, and the grander variety were worn at balls or dances. I like to imagine the wearer taking out her pencil to mark her dance card or jot down a name on the ivory pages of her notebook.

Men wore chatelaines too, with wax seals, pocket watches and knives swinging from their chain with hooks so the item could be detached, used and then reattached. However, the feminine display of charms popularized during the nineteenth century meant the chatelaine became a token of identity as much as functionality. By now the chatelaine was worn by all members of society, from royalty to aristocrats, maids and nurses, and whilst they were all the rage, some felt the number of trinkets had got out of hand. On 4 December 1897, the *Chicago Tribune* reported: 'Chatelaines are all the go again. Mother Gooses' lady who wore rings on her fingers and bells on her toes didn't begin to make the music that the up-to-date girl makes as she passes along. She wears no fewer than eight or ten jingling gimcracks attached to her chatelaine, and the consequent din in any place crowded with women reminds one of the music in a Chinese theatre.'

CHARM BRACELETS

The chatelaine allowed women to carry all the things that are important to them at once. We are lucky to have bags, so our amulets and charms are entirely light-hearted, with no practical function at all. Over time, amulets and talismans have morphed into love tokens, souvenirs and mementoes of happy times. Charm bracelets are worn to build up a life story around a wrist, commemorating a person's important moments, identity, hobbies, holidays and family. The charms are small distillations of memories and, like the tiny notebooks on the chatelaine, they became witty, amusing and cleverly crafted, like miniature toys to be admired and played with.

Speed-read the charms on a woman's wrist and they can talk you through her life, from her star sign, the time she was a bridesmaid, to every place she's visited, her pets, graduation and beyond. Everything about charms is to do with the narrative they tell, who they belong to and when they were worn. You can always also gauge the times in which a person lived by their charms. Anne Boleyn, for example, wore a small gold and enamel pistol on a chain with a snake entwined around the barrel as the earliest love token from King Henry VIII. It was a luxurious trifle but it also had a more practical function, containing a toothpick with a sickle-shaped end, a straight toothpick and a spoon for removing ear wax. For better or worse, we don't see those kinds of charms today. Nor do we see gold whistle charms in the shape of a dragon with which to summon a servant like the one worn by Sir Nicholas Bacon in 1579.

In the Elizabethan age most people believed in witches, the devil, evil spirits and magic. Queen Elizabeth I had a salamander charm, symbolic of withstanding flames, as well as a more light-hearted frog, alluding to the pet name for her French suitor, the duc d'Alençon. Queen Victoria's charm bracelet boasted sixteen lockets containing pictures of her children and locks of their hair, projecting the image of the idealized family. Following the death of her beloved husband Prince Albert she went into deep mourning and had a cast of his hand laid on the pillow next to her every night as a protective charm. Italian-born 1920s fashion designer Elsa Schiaparelli's surrealist heritage was evidenced by her miniature leek, cauliflower and aubergine charms.

In the 1940s, the actress and dancer Ginger Rogers wore charms including an old-style white telephone with a moving dial revealing the words 'I Love U' and a musical staff, no doubt alluding to the ten musicals she filmed with dancing partner Fred Astaire. Coco Chanel's superstitious nature was written all over her bracelet, which jostled with a mix of old coins hung next to Maltese crosses, lucky camellia flowers, the number 5 (her lucky number) and interlocking 'C's. The use of decorative initials on jewels originated with the idea of the monogram, a word taken from the Greek *mono*, meaning sole, and *gram*, for letter. Two or more letters were interwoven, like Chanel's double 'C's. It was the earliest form of identification used on Roman coins, with the markings of the ruler's initials. Monograms were found on everything from tablecloths to armour to designate the property of the nobility, and they became increasingly ornate. Henry VIII used a diamond-crowned monogram on his pomander and his jewels were fashioned with a large Roman-style H, occasionally emblazoned with the intertwined initial of his current wife.

Anne Boleyn, Henry VIII's second wife, famously wore a pearl necklace featuring a large 'B' in the portrait that hangs in the National Portrait Gallery in London. Everyone has their own personal cipher now, but it was a bold statement at the time. She was identifying herself as a Boleyn, declaring self-ownership at a time when women didn't have independence. Boleyn is partly remembered now as a style setter. The initial charm has lost its original use as a means to identify property, but like the way Boleyn used hers, it's a way to brand one's identity. Given that the charm bracelet is all about individuality, it's unsurprising that they sparkle with so many initials, each making small golden gestures of self-autonomy.

Elizabeth Taylor collected charms throughout her lifetime. One gold and multi-gem bracelet shone with nearly twenty charms, including a textured heart-shaped locket inscribed 'Alexandre, 60, Elysabeth Taylor', a Scorpio medallion, a bi-coloured director's slate inscribed 'The Taming of the Shrew', lockets inscribed with her children's birth dates, cartouche inscribed with the name of her chalet in Gstaad, an agate heart, an Israeli Hamsa and a Star of David. Another suspended thirty charms such as four-leaf clovers, Scorpio pendants, an evil eye, a peace symbol, a coral ankh, hearts and religious charms. Her qualities as an actress, beauty, friend, romantic figure, mother, style icon, businesswoman and humanitarian live on through these carefully sourced and deeply personal charms. What I'd give to be in a room with Elizabeth Taylor, listening to her talk me through the story of each one.

EYE CHARMS

Most of the charms mentioned thus far are either about calling in aid to fight evil spirits or using gestures to divert their attention. Elizabeth Taylor loved garnering attention, and her beauty attracted admiring gazes from anyone she met. It's interesting, then, that her charm swag included bright blue evil eyes. Although we are hardwired to feel a frisson of thrill upon capturing someone's glance and, as much as we might want to stand out, we should also be wary of the very thing we seek. Throughout history, across cultures and religions, people have feared the malevolent gaze of someone who wishes them harm.

It's important to understand the distinction between the evil glance and the evil eye, or eye amulet. The ancients believed that some malignant influence departed from the eyes of envious or angry people and infected the air to penetrate and corrupt other people's bodies, and the evil eye defeats spirits by outstaring them. The Egyptians used the sacred and unblinking Eye of Horus, with its strong eyebrow, defined eyelids and a large, round pupil, to force an evil gaze to look away; a rival eye to battle the evil one.

The Mohammedans, like the Neapolitans, are profound believers in the efficacy of manual signs; thus, outside of many a door in Tangier is the imprint of a hand made by placing the outstretched hand upon some sticky black or coloured material which was then transferred to the doorway of the dwelling, wherein the likeness of the outstretched manus serves to guard the dwellers within. I have seen a relic of the same belief over the great gate of the Alhambra, in the Tower of Justice, where, in spite of the strict Muslim custom and belief against representation of any living object, over the keystone of the outer Moorish arch is carved an outstretched upright hand, a powerful protection against evil. It is this position of the hand that has been observed in all countries in the administration of the judicial oath.

The hand in the customary position of benediction is sometimes open and extended, whilst at other times only the first and second fingers are straightened. The power which the extended hand may exert is well illustrated in the biblical account (Exodus 17:11): 'And it came to pass when Moses held up his hand that Israel prevailed, and when he let down his hand Amalek prevailed'. And so it happened that when Moses wearied of the constrained position, his hand was supported by Aaron and by Hur. This is only one of numerous illustrations in the holy writings showing the talismanic influence of the human hand.

There are comparatively few people who realize, today, that the conventional attitude of prayer as benediction, with hands held up, is the old charm against the evil eye. In one of the great marble columns in the Hagia Sophia in Istanbul there appears to be the white outline of an outspread hand upon the dark marble. This is held in the highest reverence by the superstitious populace, all of whom approach it to pray for protection from the evil eye. The open hand has also been stamped upon many a coin both in ancient and modern times, and the general prevalence of the hand as a form of door-knocker can be seen just as clearly in the ruins of Pompeii as in the modern dwelling.

The bodyguard incorporating eyes used in the Middle East is the Hand of Fatima. In this instance the hand is flat with fingers close together and is called a Hamsa – which means five, referring to the number of digits on the hand. In the Hindu religion it's called the Humsa hand, whilst in Judaism the Hamesh hand holds a sacred place. Sometimes the eye lies in the middle of the palm underneath three fingers, with two short thumbs on either side to make the design appear more symmetrical. The hand is worn to encourage patience and faithfulness combined with the protective eye to boost its power.

An all-seeing eye is the window to the soul, and some evil eye charms were worn to prevent any acts of betrayal. I don't believe so many wearers of the amulet today are looking for fidelity and faithfulness in particular, but more of a one-size-fits-all shield from general bad luck. It's a symbol that appears frequently in jewellery as well as fashion, worn by celebrities such as Gigi Hadid and Kim Kardashian, although many might not realize it is an emblematic remnant from the dawn of civilization, having maintained its hold on the imagination with a steady gaze for thousands of years.

FOUR-LEAF CLOVER CHARMS

Magical thinking has a robust role in human life. The brain is a powerful tool because our thoughts are not independent from our bodies' responses. There are complicated neurological pathways underlying the so-called placebo effect – when the brain convinces the body that a fake treatment is real. This version of positive thinking has been around for millennia, and the medical world is still figuring out how to harness it productively. Charms help us collectively to concentrate good thoughts on what we consider to be our lucky object. But believing sometimes isn't enough; we want to entice and attract good fortune to us with a charm to act as a magnet for luck. The French call it a *porte-bonheur*, which literally means 'a luck carrier'.

Plants have always played an important role in shaping society, providing clothing, shelter, remedies and poisons, serving both as ornament and as an index of wealth. Understandably, plants were often revered for their curative powers which, in time, became solidified into permanent charms that represented the particular plant, leaf or flower. The shamrock is a three-leafed clover and is known throughout the world as a symbol of Ireland. It was Ireland's patron saint Patrick who immortalized the shamrock as a sacred symbol. He arrived in Ireland on a mission to convert the country to Christianity and plucked shamrocks to represent the three aspects of the Holy Trinity. The Irish shamrock preserved in gold or silver as a charm has accompanied many Irish people as they travelled abroad.

Over the centuries, the rare clover flower with four branched leaves became a 'lucky' find. So lucky are these clovers deemed to be that even the small red beetles with black spots climbing their stalks have a reputation for luck. During the Middle Ages in Europe, swarms of aphids were destroying crops, so farmers prayed to the Virgin Mary for help. The beetles that preyed upon plant-destroying insects were subsequently named 'Our Lady's beetles' – or ladybirds, as we know them today.

'To have luck, you have to believe in luck,' was the mantra of the luxury jeweller Jacques Arpels. He would search his garden in Germigny-l'Évêque for four-leaf clovers to present to members of his staff who he felt could benefit from a little luck. His love of clovers, coupled with his admiration of the trefoil pattern in Arabic architecture, resulted in the famed 1968 design by Van Cleef & Arpels of an evocation of a four-leaf clover in gold-etched paisley-like patterns, edged in pearls and beads of gold.

The saying goes: 'One leaf for fame, one leaf for wealth, one leaf for a faithful lover and one leaf to bring glorious health', which neatly sums up the greatest fears of the human condition: insignificance, poverty, betrayal and illness. If the humble plant can dispense with these worries, it's not surprising it remains one of the most popular lucky charms in the world. Indeed, most charm bracelets twinkle with one.

ROCK CRYSTAL CHARMS

Every civilization has been drawn to rock crystal for its beauty as well as its vitality. From the beginning, its association with water frozen by the gods made it appear to possess magical qualities. Today, its reputation as a curative and for its talismanic properties remains undimmed.

Rock crystals are used in New Age healing now to help people summon the powerful energy to manifest what they want, contained in all kinds of small talismanic objects for decorative as well as spiritual purposes. Each new generation seems to be equally transfixed on the transformation of liquid matter into something solid through the action of time, which is presented in perfect geometric structure like the whorls of petals or a snow-flake. It's not always crystal clear, and most rock crystal contains an inner world of bubbles and wisps of smoke like tiny clouds, but that only adds to the evidence of its magical journey from the earth. Crystal is still used as a preventative charm against disease, panic, witchcraft and general mischief mostly in small rough shards of crystal hung on pendants and bracelets, or even carried loose in a pocket. It can help persuade the wearer that evil is at bay – and during bad days shines like a hopeful beacon urging them to see and act on the good.

Rock crystal makes a trusty companion, connecting past to present and accompanying us to new places, new situations and sea changes in our lives, and many attest to its efficacy and mood enhancing qualities. There is a plethora of rock crystal charms inspired by mythological, sacred and spiritual symbols to be worn on the outside to channel inner strength. The ancients used rock crystal, or *krystallos* as they called it, to ward off disease and pestilence, whereas now we use it to seek greater meaning and self-improvement.

In the scientific age, people might scoff at superstitious practices, but they can undoubtedly bring peace of mind, which, given the current waves of anxiety sweeping through the world we inhabit, can only be a good thing.

There are discernible beneficial effects to be found in our fascination with talismans, luck charms and the superstitious acts we sometimes reach for to ward off the caprices of fate. When faced with challenges which can seem insurmountable, anything can seem worth a go to remain calm and focused. The main purpose of everyday superstition is to give a sense of control in circumstances where it's lacking. Charms and rock crystal can lessen our stressors, providing our system with a set of responses that can positively affect our lives. Our brain is a power-ful tool, and if it accepts help is at hand from a stone or charm, then therein lies its protective value. Even if we know the charm can't perform magic, it can still support a psychological feeling that you have taken some action and this helps you to regain control. We will always face threats and problems, both real and imaginary, so call-ing in a little decorative magic to keep misfortune at bay makes a lot of sense to me. Plus, the charms speak of the rites of passage in our lives – what we believe or love or rely on at a certain point can change. Charms can act as decorative memos to ourselves of proof of a life lived to the full.

CHAPTER FIVE

BROOCHES

From its humble beginnings as an assemblage of sticks, thorns and flint, the brooch has come a long way from its origins. The brooch is unique amongst the jewels in this book because its original purpose was practical, not simply decorative: to hold two pieces of fabric together.

Brooches were an integral part of Viking dress, used as cloak fasteners. Penannular brooches, with a grooved hoop and pin fastened on the shoulder, were most likely adopted from Celtic settlers, and they featured increasingly intricate geometric patterns, depicting Norse gods such as Thor as well as animal designs. The status within the group was in many ways denoted by the levels of artistry of their ornament. Viking brooch styles dominated in Britain at the time of their invasion, and local craftsmen mimicked the design and manufacturing process used by the Vikings, but also adapted them to suit what we think of as Anglo-Saxon dress of the time, which wasn't quite the same as Scandinavian attire, so those jewels tell us about that cultural contact. Viking women favoured oval-shaped brooches to hold their garments, which meant that they wouldn't mistake a female clad with a square-shaped Anglo-Saxon-style brooch as one of their own.

The Romans used *fibulae*, ornate safety pins positioned on the right shoulder, to hold a cloak in place. The Roman historian Cassius Dio, born almost a century after Boudicca's rebellion, described the warrior queen as tall and wearing 'a tunic of diverse colours over which a thick mantle was fastened with a brooch'. In addition to such visual accounts, archaeological finds from the Iron Age and early Roman Britain have revealed a wide variety of brooches in both form and design. From their unassuming beginning, craftsmen using small chisels began to give brooches more elaborate forms, with spiralling shapes and geometric details reflecting the natural world.

Although the original purpose of brooches was practical, gradually they assumed the role of fashion accessory, and the types of clothing worn over the centuries has

This finely carved cameo brooch features the detailed profile of the ancient Greek hero Perseus, wearing scaled armour, carved through layers of light-pink sardonyx (circa 1820).

One of Queen Victoria's most beloved jewels: a coronet mounted with diamonds and sapphires. It was commissioned and designed by her husband, Prince Albert, in 1840 and is based on his coat of arms, the Saxon Rautenkranz. The coronet was immortalised in Queen Victoria's 1842 official portrait by Franz Xaver Winterhalter, becoming a symbol of both her power and love.

A gold hooped neck piece (circa 800–700 BCE), most likely used as a ceremonial collar of status and rank, found in a bog in Shannongrove, County Limerick, in 1783.

The Imperial Crown of Russia witnessed the coronation of every Russian monarch, from Catherine the Great in 1762 until the abdication of Tsar Nicholas II in 1917, which marked the end of the Empire and the ruling Romanov dynasty.

Giardinetti (meaning 'little garden') designs, in the form of bouquets, posies and floral arrangements, became popular in 1750. This brooch (circa. 1890) has tiny gems set as blooms organised asymmetrically in woven baskets, stone pots and vases.

Early eighteenth-century European glass beads created in Venice were known as 'trade' or 'slave' beads, as glass formed a major part of the currency exchange for people and products in West Africa.

This ornate golden 'halo' of wide hoops and a headdress of gold leaves, lapis lazuli and carnelian was found with the body of Queen Puabi inside a vaulted chamber in the Royal Tombs at Ur.

This pectoral necklace (circa 1887–1878 BCE), found in the tomb
of Princess Sithathoryunet, is inlaid with 372 semi-precious stones.

The style of this Girandole brooch (circa 1835) mimics the
branched shape of a candelabra. The central motif – three suspended
pear-shaped peridot stones, which would sparkle beautifully in
candlelight – gives it the name 'evening emeralds'.

Nature as we know it is expressed in these Byzantine gold hoops,
featuring blue, green and white cloisonné enamel birds on twigs
and branches, radiating with pearls and gold pyramids.

An eighteenth-century ivory cylindrical arm cuff, inlaid with gilded brass
and carved with repeated designs of European heads, was made by Edo
jewellers in Benin City. The solid cylindrical cuff would be worn by the
'Oba' or ruler, adorned with copious strings of beads.

One of Queen Victoria's most sentimental pieces: an orange blossom headdress in gold, enamel and porcelain, gifted by her husband in 1846 on their sixth wedding anniversary. She continued to wear elements of this orange blossom parure to celebrate anniversaries throughout their married life.

A brightly coloured Anglo-Saxon disc brooch (circa 600AD). These gold filigree patterns and polished garnets reflect the high quality of objects worn by individuals at the time.

This gold Claddagh ring was made in Galway, Ireland, in the mid-seventeenth century. The two hands holding a crowned heart symbolize the union of marriage, with the coronet over the heart denoting the supreme power of love.

Pomanders filled with sweet-smelling herbs and spices were used from the late Middle Ages as a way for ladies to combat noxious smells and protect themselves from disease. This Renaissance-style eighteenth-century pomander may have been fitted with a glass liner containing soap to emit a fragrant incense.

impacted the way brooches were fashioned at any given period in history. For one, the weight and thickness of the material dictated how heavy a brooch could be. So, for example, the massive diamond stomachers worn on the front of a bodice during the eighteenth century suited court robes and ball gowns constructed at the time from heavy silk brocades and damask. When silk and light tulle swept into fashion in the neo-classical age, there was literally no longer a place for such a weighty ornament, and brooches became smaller and more discreet.

Brooches had this practical function, but they also served as markers of identity. They are expressive pieces of personal ornamentation, used for centuries to communicate ideas about everything from personality to social status and broader political and cultural ideas. Largely, though, brooches have been an effective method of communicating visually what cannot be vocalized directly.

Coco Chanel said that brooches elevated both the costume and the woman wearing it, and they form a key part of a woman's wardrobe who wants her views known. The artistry and craftsmanship of the brooch is on show every bit as much as the meaning the wearer wants to express, which could be a personal statement about character or the larger intention of voicing support of a global event.

Whilst we might think of brooches as something worn by older generations, on TikTok, videos tagged #brooch have garnered more than 100 million views. During lockdown, the rise of Zoom calls emphasized the desire for jewellery that has visual impact and can be easily spotted on screen. It seems that even in our era of minimalism, we can't resist a sparkly accessory. Indeed, Gucci saw a 70 per cent rise in demand for their pins over Christmas 2022 and other designers like Saint Laurent and Jil Sander are getting in on the brooch action too.

GIRANDOLES

Since the Renaissance, the central panel of a dress bodice, called a stomacher, was richly decorated with precious stones and pearls sewn onto the fabric. During the eighteenth century, ornamental eye-catching jewels were pinned onto the bodice. Made of gold and silver, they were effectively large, richly decorated brooches, and their weight meant they could only be pinned to a bodice if it was corseted. Like the tiara, they were worn at formal events to show off one's status and wealth.

Lavish brooch designs developed the shape of the bow, featuring three pear-shaped pendants, mimicking the branched girandole support for candles which rested on tables or projected light from a wall. The brooch would be secured onto corseted bodices, and sometimes smaller girandole versions would be scattered over the rest of the outfit. They were most striking when the wearer twirled around candlelit ballrooms and cast dazzling lights from the moving jewels. The importance of light, and therefore candelabra, to the Georgians epitomized more than anything else the taste and style of the period.

High society had a passion for costume balls, gossip, flirting and dancing at night-time soirées lit by beeswax candles. The girandole ornament is redolent of this important development of Georgian lighting at the time. The simplest form of candle was a rush light, a dried rush dipped in animal fat and clipped on a mounted stand. A more expensive variety was the animal fat tallow candle, but both options burned badly and smelled unpleasant. Beeswax candles were the preferred option, but only the wealthy could afford to banish the gloom using these with abandon. In 1712, it was reported that the Duchess of Montagu paid £200 for candles for an assembly lasting one night, whilst another claim stated the Duke of Bedford used over 1,000 candles to illuminate a single evening. Regardless of the economics, improved lighting meant more social occasions could be held at night, which suited the girandole brooch and earrings. In due course, the government began taxing the candles so the cost of lighting a grand dinner became exorbitant.

Girandole brooches remained in fashion until the advent of electric lighting at the beginning of the twentieth century. In a way, the girandole takes us back to another time and speaks of societal changes encompassing the history of lighting, with drops of diamond light sparkling like fireworks. Many were broken up when they finally went out of fashion, but occasionally I still spot watered-down versions of the girandole, particularly in earrings, which have been diluted through the years by designers who couldn't begin to know the difference a bright girandole would have made in its heyday.

LITTLE GARDENS

Flowers, plants and garden landscape design have influenced jewellery from the beginning. Jewellers have gone beyond replicating a single brilliant specimen to finding stimulus in the way different generations plan, cultivate, display and enjoy plants and other forms of nature. A cross-fertilization of ideas has entwined garden design with jewels; both react to historical events, fashions and technological advances as certain styles are swept away in favour of new attitudes, romanticism or freshly introduced gemstones and hybrid species. Certain periods of garden design are expressed in jewels sharing a type of texture, pattern and shape as well as the enthusiasm for contrasts and colour, offering a visualization of the changing fashions in scenery and gardens.

Until the latter part of the eighteenth century, gardens were planted with formality, order and strict symmetry, as exemplified by the gardens of Versailles. A new taste and fashion emerged as interest grew in country houses and gardens, particularly for what the French dubbed the *jardin anglais*. The countryside became one with the house, with the idea to give uninterrupted views, which led to vibrant plants and exotic trees framing garden views, punctuated by classical temples, grottos, sculptures and urns. The artist Thomas Gainsborough described these decorative objects as 'a little business for the Eye'.

The fashion for the English landscape garden swept through Europe, America and as far east as Russia. These pleasure gardens with a focus on more naturalistic designs were reflected in the new trend for *giardinetti* or 'little garden' brooches of tiny blossoms arranged with rococo asymmetry in diamond tied bouquets, vases and baskets. *Giardinetti* became eye-catchers worn on new countrified day dresses as women everywhere walked outside to enjoy the natural world. Some of these flowers were created with colourful gemstones or foil-backed diamonds to emulate soft pastel shades. Sometimes they were tied with a diamond ribbon bow, whilst some brooches featured tiny gemstone flowers 'planted' in pots, baskets and precious urns, mimicking the large classic stone urns punctuating terraces and landscape gardens all over the country. Stems were enamelled or fashioned from green emeralds with larger flower heads set on springs so they could tremble and glitter as the wearer moved.

Little garden brooches spread through the fashionable world like a breath of fresh country air, often exchanged as love tokens between couples or friends. Presenting someone you admired with a bouquet of flowers that would endure was all the rage. During the 1920s, the fashion returned for *giardinetti* brooches in the form of art deco-style lapis lazuli urns filled with leaf-shaped engraved rubies, diamonds and onyx beads, which were inspired by miniature Japanese bonsai trees. Bonsai cultivation was practised in China as early as the fourth century BCE by Taoists who believed that recreating nature in miniature yielded magical benefits and by Zen Buddhists who believed that bonsai were objects of meditation.

To celebrate the birth of Prince Charles in 1948, Queen Elizabeth II was given a flower basket brooch. It was one of the most colourful brooches in her vast collection and features ruby, diamond and sapphire gemstones.

During the Covid-19 lockdown I noticed contemporary versions of these *giardinetti* cropping up as people at home in urban environments began to thirst for the natural world. More generally, as our population increases and cities dominate the landscape, society's relationship with gardening has adapted. For a large percentage of city dwellers, the environmental benefits of restoring nature to our urban surroundings, paired with a desire to reconnect with nature, has led to a renewed interest in planting green spaces. Every inch of outside areas and patios is being used to place a pot plant or window box to satisfy our primitive desire of watching things grow. Cora Sheibani's new collection, 'Pottering Around', features gem-set jewels designed as potted plants like modern *giardinetti*, as well as Taffin's ever-green, emerald cacti blossoming with spinel flowers and planted in jasper pots, exemplifying how society gardens now, in small spaces on windowsills and patio terraces.

Protest badges

History attests to the brooch's long association with politics, from revolutionary movements to demonstrations for equality and innumerable other causes. The designs of many brooches residing in museums are historical missives still proudly parading their role in bygone disputes, although the causes in some cases remain relevant.

Brooches have been vital tools to foster solidarity between groups with the same ideology and purpose. Even if a person felt powerless in promoting the change required, by donning a brooch they could feel they were doing their bit. In the age of social media, it's easy to understand the power of a potent image and how it quickly identifies the beliefs of the 'tribe' you belong to. Think of the red-ribbon-style pins we wore to align ourselves with the victims of the HIV/AIDs epidemic. Brooches can be quickly produced to comment on current events, a phenomenon that was particularly successful in the pre-internet age, when an issue could be widely disseminated, increasing its importance to provoke political discussion.

In 1787, when women pinned certain jasperware medallion brooches in their hair, they were showing their support for the anti-slavery campaign. These oval white plaques depicted a black enslaved man, in the act of praying, his hands clasped together, his arms chained to his legs, his right knee to the ground, with the moulded letters above, 'Am I not a man and your brother'. The image was taken from the seal of the London-based Society for Effecting the Abolition of the Slave Trade, founded by Thomas Clarkson and Granville Sharp, and the medallion brooches became an emblem of the anti-slavery movement in Britain, France and the United States.

The English potter and abolitionist Josiah Wedgwood produced and distributed the brooches and one example remains in the British Royal Collection. A consignment was sent to Benjamin Franklin, whilst serving as president of the Pennsylvania Abolition Society, who wrote of the effectiveness of the image that it was 'equal to that of the best written Pamphlet, in procuring favour to those oppressed People.' As they say, a picture is worth a thousand words.

The medallions were distributed there amongst abolitionists and anti-slavery campaigners, and Clarkson reported on their success, 'some had them inlaid in gold on the lid of their snuffboxes. Of the ladies, several wore them in bracelets, and others had them fitted up in an ornamental manner as pins for their hair. At length the taste for wearing them became general, and thus fashion ... was seen for once in the honourable office of promoting the cause of justice, humanity and freedom.'

The number of medallions produced was made possible

by Wedgwood's pioneering techniques, using steam power to drive the pottery polishing machines – an early system of mass production. So, the ceramic brooch became a unifying message for white abolitionists whilst they petitioned Parliament to end the slave trade. Wearing the brooch also encouraged them to drop exotic sugar from their diet. The fashion for tea, coffee and chocolate, which tasted bitter on their own, accelerated the demand for sugar, which in turn fuelled the demand for enslaved labour on sugar plantations in the West Indies. These anti-saccharites recognized the inter-connectedness of Empire and global consumption, so boycotted sugar for its connections to enslaved labour.

In more recent times, the Black Lives Matter movement has also been about the politicization of protest, and although sadly we don't have a new emblem to flaunt on our lapels, the Wedgwood medallion and its historic and contemporary meanings are being looked at again, remaking the icon into an empowering object for the twenty-first century.

The Covid-19 pandemic had a regressive effect on gender equality, especially for women of colour. It's International Women's Day as I write, and an email has pinged into my inbox stating that 2.4 billion women of working age are not afforded equal economic opportunity. And that's only one area of many that impacts women's lives.

Could it be time to don a suffragette brooch again

to defend women's rights? Thousands of women were imprisoned fighting for equality and political rights during the Victorian era and most of them sported a brooch in the campaign's colours of white, green and lavender to declare their political intention. By 1903, the brooch had become a mission statement advertising membership of the Women's Social and Political Union founded by activist Emmeline Pankhurst. Their brooches were fashioned in enamel, with emerald, amethyst and pearl representing hope, dignity and purity, voicing the courage of these women who were willing to use every weapon in their arsenal, from petitions and speeches to pins, parades and attention-grabbing stunts.

Emmeline Pethick-Lawrence, the treasurer of the Women's Social and Political Union, devised the group's colour scheme with the aim of politicizing appearance, so suffragettes could easily spot one another in the street. The brooch became an important tool in their dress as well as in the fight for equality. Called 'Votes for Women' pins, they sometimes took the shape of a heart set with green peridot, pearls and purple amethyst. White, green and purple was the best-known colour scheme adopted by the WSPU, but other groups also devoted to the suffrage cause adopted a wider colour palette. Before they reached a demonstration, women could gather together and recognize each other by their badges of solidarity pinned to a dress or jacket.

A different brooch was worn as a badge of honour,

presented to women who'd served prison time for their actions during protests. Named 'the Holloway Brooch' after the London prison where adult women offenders were incarcerated, it was designed by campaigning feminist Sylvia Pankhurst with a portcullis (the symbol of Parliament), overlaid with a three-pronged arrow (associated with prison uniforms), in white, green and purple enamel. Hunger Strike Medals were also worn to draw attention to the bravery of the wearer who had undergone the barbaric practice of force feeding.

Shining from women's lapels during open-air meetings and parades, the brooches were instrumental as objects of commitment that helped keep suffragettes focused on the long road to suffrage and aided in the spread of the message, appealing to working women to join the cause to improve their conditions. 'By the turn of the century, you had, in New York City, 30,000 marchers and half a million onlookers,' the *New York Times* reported, who went on to warn that if women did achieve the vote, it would play havoc with society, 'they would demand all the rights that implies. It is not possible to think of women as soldiers, sailors, police, patrolmen or firemen.' Women who couldn't risk the police brutality, assault and arrest that some campaigning attracted sported their brooches in the spirit of camaraderie. When it wasn't appropriate for a woman to espouse her opinion, a simple brooch was all she needed to voice her belief in parliamentary change.

Recently, there's been a reversal of circumstances,

as a brooch itself has become the subject of protest. 'Blackamoor' brooches feature stylized African men and women wearing jewelled turbans and richly decorated costumes. These elaborately robed figures became a trope in Italian decorative art. The motif emerged as a response to the Moors, Muslims from North Africa and the Middle East who arrived in Europe during the Middle Ages. Popular from the sixteenth to the nineteenth century, they are now considered racist objects. Outrage exploded on social media sites when Princess Michael of Kent was pictured wearing one to the late Queen's Christmas lunch at Windsor Castle. She issued a formal apology. None was required when Dame Shirley Bassey wore one in 2023 at the opening party of the V&A Museum's Diva exhibition.

In Italy, the brooches are called called *moretti*, referring to William Shakespeare's legendary figure Othello, 'the Moor of Venice'. Each is unique and created with faces of ebony swathed in golden turbans worked like moire silk, bedecked with egret plumes above torsos made of ornamental stones, cameos or intaglios. The tradition survives in Venice where Moorish heads look out from jewellers' windows around St Mark's Square as sculpted objects of luxury once bought by Princess Grace, Elizabeth Taylor and Jacqueline Onassis. To others they are offensive badges perpetuating racist tropes and the costumes on these figures emphasize the popular trend of European fetishization of 'exotic' appearances.

ART MODERNE

In May 1929, the Union des Artistes Modernes was founded by an influential group of modernist decorative artists and architects who were disillusioned with the conservative Societé des Artistes Décorateurs from which they split. These *bijoutiers-artistes* espoused the radical point of view that bejewelled ornamentation didn't have a monopoly on beauty and were on a quest for newness, determined to make a major impact on jewellery's aesthetic. Jean Fouquet was amongst the founding members of this movement, together with Gérard Sandoz and Raymond Templier. The mission was to abandon past traditions and focus on design, reducing jewels to the most essential forms, referencing the new machine age. The art moderne movement was born and brooches became a revolutionary symbol once again.

In their opinion jewellery wasn't expressing modern life, and they wanted to make pieces that reflected the true spirit of the age. Their artistic creations strove for modernity in powerful and original pieces, and the principal characteristic they sought to inject into their work was speed. Jewels, therefore, had the metallic glint and sense of movement that reflected the new automobiles that were gracing the roads at the time. Henry Ford's advances in assembly-line efficiency made the black Model T Ford a thrilling new experience which became part of everyday life, whilst car racing captured the public interest and garnered numerous headlines. Charles Lindbergh became the first person to fly solo between New York and Paris, whilst civilian aviation was setting records all the time.

'As I walk in the streets, I see ideas for jewellery everywhere,' explained Templier, 'the wheels, the cars, the machinery of today'. His experiences of the world gave him and his colleagues a whole new visual language and an aesthetic where strong, powerful forms replaced any intricacy or representational motifs and compositions. Rather, they used abstract motifs, geometric shapes and sleek lines to break away from the glamorous and excessively bejewelled designs that had been popular during the 1920s.

Geometric shapes fashioned from onyx, silver, gold and semi-precious stones with minimal use of precious gems were the preferred choices. These were created as works of art as opposed to financial investments. Brooches were attached to cloche hats or worn on the shoulder or the belt of a tunic. The daring women who wore the first female tuxedos used geometric pins as decoration.

French designer Jean Després served as a mechanic and draughtsman in the air force during the First World War, which informed his style of jewellery design for the rest of his life. Many of his pieces were influenced by engine parts, such as his 'Connecting Rod' and 'Camshaft' brooches. He saw the beauty in machines, mechanical shapes, tubing, crankshafts and all sort of elements of machinery reimagined mostly in silver with harmony of line, a sense of proportion and volume, and a level of craftsmanship.

Some of Després' brooches were made of little plates of square metal and often comprised overlapping layers decorated with lacquered geometric elements or an inlay of hard stones like lapis lazuli or malachite.

'I love metal. You have no idea what pleasure it gives me to see the material bend under the anvil and hear it grate in the vice. I tame it but without breaking it. The idea is to leave all its vitality and suppleness intact,' reported Després, who wasn't dependent on the price of materials or the size of gemstone. 'The science of mechanics imposes a wholly modern discipline to cope with the rejection of anything useless or complicated.'

Some were scandalized at the time, as no one had dared before to create jewels that reproduced pistons, ball bearings, camshafts and connecting rods, yet his work wholly embodied the modern ideal of the age.

In the 1920s, the machine represented liberation and was about as central to life as you could say technology is today. Life today is also about speed and whilst we are witnessing designs using discarded elements of iPhones and computers and brooches inspired by pixels, so far, the digital age hasn't produced a revolutionary new movement in jewellery design. As yet, I don't feel one style has embodied the modern ideal of our age. The beauty of art moderne lives on and, in my eyes, still conjures up excitement, the essence of movement and of life changing. The art moderne movement was on the cutting edge of technical experimentation and created pieces that even now, 100 years later, are striking in their originality.

PATRIOTIC BROOCHES

During the First and Second World Wars, brooches became less about design and more about demonstration. They were worn by women as an expression of patriotism and a sign that their family were 'doing their bit' for the war effort. Flags, regimental badges, pins and lockets and other patriotic symbols were worn as unifying jewels. Often 'sweetheart' brooches were replicas of badges of military regiments, naval units, the Royal Flying Corps and the RAF, and given as keepsakes to mothers, wives and girlfriends before their menfolk left home to fight. They were symbols of solidarity and patriotism as well as signs of devotion and love. In this way, a small, inexpensive brooch made a visible and tangible link between front-line personnel and families at home – something to hold onto as a talisman in the hope it would generate good luck and bring the soldier home safely, thereby reuniting the brooch and the original insignia that inspired it. In the US, women proudly wore 'man in service' brooches with a blue star on a white background with a red enamelled border to indicate they had a family member at war.

Flags waved from lapels as did other costume jewels which were inspired by the symbols, colours and

iconography of American history. Old Glory, the nick-
name for the flag of the United States, alongside other
nationalistic emblems such as Uncle Sam's hat, the Liberty
Bell, the torch of the Statue of Liberty and various impressive American-styled eagles soon flourished in the form
of brooches. Men restricted from fighting pinned small
aircraft or miniature white uniformed sailors heading off
to battle in their jackets, proudly proclaiming a belief and
solidarity in the armed forces and devotion to country.
And everyone chose their brooches according to their economic situation, right the way from cheap buttons bought
on street corners to precious gem-set brooches. The British
and French flags were also in demand at this time, along
with 'God Bless America' and red, white and blue enamel
and rhinestone bowknots.

Other dainty pins were fashioned in Winston
Churchill's iconic 'V for victory', making a subtle yet clear
political statement. This became a symbol of hope and a
call to action, inspiring not only the British, but also the
Americans, Dutch and French. Another ornament was
a bracelet brooch with miniature flags and emblems of
the Allied Powers, which was a brief show of solidarity
amongst several nations, some of whom would later
become Cold War adversaries.

Jewellery was considered patriotic even when it was
not emblematic, but merely displayed the Allied colours
of red, white and blue picked out in enamel, crystals or
stones. In 1940, Lord Beaverbrook launched the 'Spitfire

Fund' to raise funds to save and source raw materials all in aid of the war effort. A figure of £5,000 was set as the target for each plane, funded in part by the production of Spitfire buttons and badges for the public to buy as a way of encouraging morale and a feeling of achievement for the nation.

Most jewellery factories in Britain were requisitioned for the manufacture of munitions and radio parts, and since European crystals were in short supply and base metals were rationed, designers made creative use of Bakelite, Lucite and other low-cost materials. The production of non-essential jewellery was prohibited by the Control of Manufacture and Supply Orders. In 1941, it was stated that only necessary items could be produced, which comprised identification bracelets, cufflinks, studs and wedding rings, and then only under licence. The wartime attitude of 'make do and mend' applied to jewellery as well as clothes.

In Germany during the First World War, gold jewels were donated to the war effort. Throughout history jewels have been requisitioned as a patriotic duty to fund warfare. The Fascist dictator Benito Mussolini appealed to the patriotism of Italian wives, asking them to swap their gold wedding rings for steel versions to raise funds. Those who didn't contribute were publicly shamed and in the end 33.622 tons of gold were eventually melted down and deposited in banks. The replacement steel bands were inscribed with *Oro alla Patria* – 'gold for the fatherland'.

This drive could have been inspired by an early patriotic appeal in 1813 when Prussia was at war with France and and Princess Marianne of Prussia urged Prussian women to donate their gold to fund the war against Napoleon Bonaparte. Anyone who responded received iron jewellery in exchange, which was often a brooch, each piece inscribed with *Gold gab ich für Eisen* – 'I gave gold for iron'.

In 1942, Cartier created a brooch in the form of a caged bird following the Nazi invasion of France, in protest of the occupation. Following the liberation of Paris, another brooch was created depicting a jubilant bird in coral, diamond and lapis lazuli, singing in an open cage, poised for flight and freedom.

Production of patriotic jewels tailed off after the end of the Second World War, but they are still worn today as a show of national solidarity following recent conflicts and events such as the Gulf War and the 9/11 terrorist attacks. In the US, a stars-and-stripes flag pin remains the favoured method of visible patriotism in a time of threat. For instance, when Nancy Pelosi, the former speaker of the House of Representatives, was announcing the formal impeachment inquiry of former President Donald Trump, a large flag sparkled against her dark suit. The president himself often wore a similar flag in his buttonhole, however, the larger size of Pelosi's spoke volumes about the perception of their respective levels of patriotism and love of country.

DANCING BROOCHES

Women had taken important roles during the war, especially on the 'home front', in fields, factories and other civil work. During the war years, brooches hadn't been restricted to the precious variety for the elite; they were for everyone. Although the magnitude of post-war upheaval affected every aspect of society, ultimately freedom beckoned, and women wanted to celebrate by wearing an object that embodied their newfound independence and continued existence in the face of adversity. The brooch became the fashionable accessory of the day, and the masculine clothes worn by working women required heavier pieces to sit on the wide lapel of a tailored jacket. Bigger was therefore better, and nothing was deemed too sparkly or opulent. Designers were using new enriching motifs depicting popular culture in colour, and brooches had a 'feel good' quality, worn to show off humour and whimsy, satisfying a thirst for brightness and escapism that brought some much-needed sparkle and levity into fashion.

Societal changes for women meant they generally spent more time working outside the home becoming economically independent, and they sought to spend their money on something decorative but also out of the ordinary that would reflect their personality. They also wanted a little Hollywood glamour in their lives, and costume jewelled brooches became important symbols of their style. Many were beautifully crafted, incorporating the finesse and detail of Parisian fine jewels. Over the war years, America had been flooded with artists in exile, including émigré jewellery manufacturers who settled in the US and continued to practise the fine jewellery techniques they'd learnt in Europe on non-precious materials. These designers who'd fled war-torn Europe were eager for a glittering reminder of Old World art. Bijou jewellery was now fashioned like a precious jewel, whilst resonating with a new sense of frivolity and freedom. Women were ready for entertainment and a fresh point of view and brooches provided just the ticket.

Designers in America had a freedom to experiment, creating miniature cowboys throwing a gilt rope lasso, alongside comic book characters and Disney cartoon animals with detailed moving parts, so they appeared almost animated. These were clipped like tiny playthings to dresses. It was new style that demonstrated American culture, never previously explored in jewellery. At the time in New York, nightclubs such as El Morocco and the Stork Club were filled with people dancing. The seductive rhythms of Latin dances such as the rumba and samba were new to the United States, and the mood was reflected in a profusion of dancing jewels.

Italian-born designer Gustavo Trifari closely observed the movement of dancers and produced bright jewelled costume jewellery featuring characters such as Russian Cossack dancers or a couple swaying in unison wearing Spanish flamenco dress. In time, he created an entire corps de ballet, with tiny ballerinas pirouetting in fluted gilt-metal skirts, fashioned to look like swirling pleated fabric.

On the Lower East Side of Manhattan, Van Cleef & Arpels' manufacturer John Rubel frequented a café to watch the flamenco dancers. In 1942, the French jewellery *maison* had opened their doors in New York City for the first time and, with designer Maurice Duvalet, Rubel created a sparkling troupe of female dancers. Claude Arpels, president of the company, had a fascination with the art of dance, forming a close friendship with ballet choreographer George Balanchine, and his visits to the ballet inspired the *maison*'s first jewelled ballerina brooch. She was followed by generations of jewelled ballerinas, pirouetting and twirling with upturned rose-cut diamond faces and precious headdresses. Many of the figures are depicted with point shoes and a tutu made of diamonds or coloured stones that seem to flow, echoing the dancers' movements.

The realistic poses of the jewelled dancers were mimicked from watching ballet rehearsals, paintings or photographs of prima ballerina Anna Pavlova's *Dying Swan* performance, who was one of the first ballerinas to tour the world with the Imperial Russian Ballet. A who's who of American fashionistas sported the little masterworks, including Barbara Hutton, Elizabeth Taylor and Marjorie Merriweather Post. Cossack dancers have since been added to the *oeuvre*, high kicking in bright yellow sapphires, amethysts and moonstones, as well as dancing princesses inspired by Grimms' 'The Twelve Dancing Princesses'. Not only do the poses and costumes change for each ballerina, but each one of the jewels shines with an individual personality. Now, changing tastes have transformed some of the diamond-studded ballerinas into vibrant three-dimensional figures, some with a sharper edge.

PANTHERS

Following the Second World War, women had gained a new sense of power, having been conscripted into work of national importance breaking codes, tracking battleships and driving trucks. They exploded the myth, as written in the *New York Times*, that, as the 'fairer sex', they weren't up to it. The divorce rate rocketed for many reasons, but one was that women now believed they could be permitted a say in their own destiny. These women were strong, feminine and independent.

Presciently, jeweller Louis Cartier began to design a new style of jewel to suit these women – albeit on a grandiose scale. His clients weren't activists and nor were these protest brooches. His was a pursuit of beauty and artistry in design, fashioned to exemplify their newfound female power, spirit and personality. In direct contrast to suffragette brooches, which you can pick up in flea markets, these are some of the most lavish and valuable ever created. In hindsight, it's hard to imagine how these brooches expressed a message of modernity, worn as they were by women whose lives were splendidly cushioned by wealth, but at the time that's just what they did.

Figurative animals are a mainstay of the jeweller's art. Nowadays many women inspired by the Native American culture seek to wear a sort of 'spirit animal', a creature they connect with, in a way that exists at the crossroads of symbolism, nature and wellness, on brooches that communicate their values.

At the end of the war, Cartier believed the panther was the best animal to convey the female power of its clients. The panthers began as an illusion of onyx spots against diamonds and slowly evolved. By 1948, the panther had reached legendary status in the form of a diamond figurative cat with sapphire spots atop of a 116.74-carat emerald which was created for the Duchess of Windsor. In due course, the Duchess amassed a cat menagerie overseen by a diamond queen with yellow diamond eyes resting on a 152-carat rock of sapphire.

Society women followed suit and soon heiresses Daisy Fellowes and Barbara Hutton sported panther and tiger brooches. Cats were the accessory *du jour* amongst the world's best dressed women and were used as an emblem exemplifying a certain type of strength and power – albeit for an elite group of women. The panther emphasized the wearer's avant-garde nature and by wearing it, women sought to capture the sense of that animal's free spirit. Also, brooches were the height of fashion and were no longer confined to decorating a lapel; they were sprinkled liberally on hair, pinned to the straps of gowns, necklines of dresses, collars and even gloves. Scores of matching clips were attached either side of square-cut necklines.

Arguably, a series of big cats was the most iconic line of jewellery created by the legendary design director of Cartier Jeanne Toussaint, whose interest in panthers was sparked following a trip to Africa in 1913. Her Parisian apartment was littered with animal skins. She'd designed several panther objects for herself, including a cigarette case, and was convinced that bejewelled panthers would captivate the hearts of a new pack of women like herself who were ready to defy convention. One journalist at the time described the impact of the ground-breaking panther as 'an atomic bomb' sitting in Cartier's shop window. The panther dominated contemporary taste of the time and remains one of the most iconic animal designs of the twentieth century. And, like the ballerinas, each panther seems to have its own expression and personality.

Choosing an animal jewel that matches you is about more than aesthetics; it becomes about what the animal represents. Just as fashion holds up a mirror to changing times, so does jewellery, which follows the tone of each era. Whilst women are still drawn to the animal they feel will represent their feelings, they also look for one that will present a moral lesson – a fox for wisdom and opportunity or a hare meaning balance. They no longer restrict themselves to handsome and noble beasts, and animal brooches shine with inclusivity and diversity. There is no creature deemed too deadly, ugly or insignificant to escape the jeweller's *oeuvre*, as we've witnessed with Bibi van der Velden's slugs and golden-scaled alligators with tsavorite eyes. These aren't just jewels; they are friends and protectors and become part of the wearer's identity.

That said, I do think this is an opportune moment to return to a wild cat or elephant brooch to send a message about conservation. *Homo sapiens* far outweighs large wild mammals, with a biomass of 390 million tons versus 22 million tons. In fact, the biomass of domestic cats is double that of wild African elephants. Alternatively, perhaps a large fish brooch should come to the fore in protest of rivers full of effluent and oceans teeming with plastic.

BUG BROOCHES

As we know, jewellery is never made in isolation, and currently we are seeing a plethora of jewelled bugs and creepy-crawlies in brooches, reflecting concern about the worldwide decline in insect species caused by loss of habitat, light pollution, microplastics, synthetic pesticides and climate change. Given insects create the biological foundation for all terrestrial ecosystems, the jeweller's inspiration is drawing attention to their plight and, as a result, our own. Bees are some of the most important pollinators in the ecosystem, and without these insects we wouldn't be able to grow most of the plants we rely on to survive. Nor would those plants be able to reproduce. Gold and diamond honeybees aren't merely included in many jewellers' designs, but a percentage of sales is usually donated to bee-friendly trusts and charities. New York jeweller Marla Aaron even keeps bees, giving out the honey she produces from hives kept on her New York City roof in Harlem.

Beautiful insects such as butterflies and dragonflies have always featured in jewellery and brooches, appearing with outspread enamelled wings seemingly in motion, as if alighting for a second on a lapel, before flying away. Now, however, there's a new predilection for stag beetles, spiders, ants, flies, centipedes and ladybirds, which march like an ugly-bug army out of the jewellers' workshops. No insect is too unattractive, insignificant or lowly to have been recreated in sparkling detail by the jeweller's art.

In a decorative way, these bugs make a political point, drawing attention to the challenges of our generation. One of the most heralded uses of a 'bug' brooch to make a political argument was a large spider brooch worn by Baroness Hale, the United Kingdom's first female Law Lord and president of the Supreme Court until 2020, when she announced that Prime Minister Boris Johnson's decision to prorogue Parliament was unlawful. Her choice that day to wear a spider sparked a rash of theories as to what the symbolism meant, and it became a viral and fashion sensation. Wearing a spider to deliver a message that trapped the prime minister seemed pointed. Was it a metaphor backed on a pin about spinning webs of deceit?

Baroness Hale maintains it was not. However, the giant spider pinned to her austere black dress had the optics that made it a story of its own. Inevitably, there were soon calls for the spider to have its own Twitter account.

High-profile women since the time of Boudicca have used the brooch to project power and authority and as an avatar for their frame of mind. Madeleine K. Albright, the secretary of state under President Bill Clinton, detailed her brooch communiques in a book, *Read My Pins: Stories From a Diplomat's Jewel Box*. An avid brooch collector, her pins delivered a message about how she was feeling on any given day. So, a contentious encounter when she needed to do a little 'stinging' and deliver a tough message called for a wasp brooch. After the Russians were caught tapping the US State Department, she appeared wearing a giant bug on her left shoulder, announcing her disapproval without a word being spoken. The media are now on permanent 'brooch watch', and every time a high-profile woman wears a pin a meaning – intentional or not – is deciphered. The brooch, so to speak, has been unpinned.

Recently, a slew of Hollywood actors have set off quite a trend by wearing gem-set brooches on the red carpet through award seasons. They break up the boredom of a black tuxedo and make a style statement, but on the whole they aren't modern. Timothée Chalamet appears in a rotation of antique Cartier, and a Jean Schlumberger Bird on a Rock – or two, as worn by Michael Jordan to the Academy Awards – is also popular.

In the week following the death of Queen Elizabeth, when the family were still in mourning, the Queen Consort appeared at a luncheon wearing a diamond moth brooch with emerald eyes, which dazzled against her black dress. In some cultures, the moth signifies change, transformation and resurrection, which could have been an acknowledgement of the enormous adjustment taking place as her husband ascended the throne as King.

Lady Gaga's message as she stepped up to the rostrum to sing the national anthem at President Biden's inauguration was easy for anyone to decipher. It was a message to make peace with each other. The appliqué-like dove carrying an olive branch, custom fitted to her bust, quivered slightly as if coming alive. Emblematic of that moment, nothing else could have made that statement with such clear efficiency. No tweet could compare.

SPIRIT LEVEL BROOCH

Not every brooch is tasked with speculation on global events, politics or international relations – some monitor the ups and downs in our own personal world. 'A balancing act' is a common response when women are asked to describe their lives, whether in the public eye or not. The pressure to achieve a happy and stress-free life is enormous, and we all struggle to achieve it. Modern life imposes many demands on us. Women dash between work, family duties, housekeeping and perhaps taking care of elderly parents as well as being expected to find the time to exercise and nurture friendships. The time in the day simply runs out.

Maintaining balance between different strands of daily life is a challenge and one that jeweller Dorothy Hogg explored in a 'Spirit Level' brooch made in 1993, housed in London's Goldsmiths' Company Collection. 'The reason for making things often reveals itself in the process of making it. My work is led by my subconscious preoccupations,' Hogg explained at the time. 'My life was very busy as I had a full-time job as Head of the Department of Jewellery and Silversmithing at Edinburgh College of Art; pressure was on to create a collection of work for a solo exhibition. I had a young family and an ageing mother who needed support. Life was a balancing act.'

A tear-drop-shaped silver frame balances a line of small oval rings hanging within the tear drop. Move too fast and the rings slide to one end; balance yourself and they gather back into the centre. Hogg was experimenting with the idea of movement and change. A spirit level tool indicates whether a surface is level relative to the earth; the brooch also measures the level of a spirit. An idea that resonates with most women.

Whilst still adored by royalty and the Hollywood elite, brooches are experiencing a sort of renaissance. Recently, #bringbackthebrooch has been trending, and during the past few seasons I have also spotted more and more brooches turning up on the runway, worn in the hair, on the neckline, pinned to the waist of dresses and scattered over all styles of jackets. They are edging their way back on the fashion scene and are visible in high jewellery collections once more.

CHAPTER SIX

CUFFS

Early cuffs are the iconography of power. The ancient Egyptians, early Greeks and Romans developed the cuff as a marker of rank and status as well as armour for protection. Wrist apparel has developed into three distinct jewels: the bracelet, which has hinges and attachments to secure it to the wrist; the rigid, slim circle of a bangle; and the cuff, which isn't a perfect circle but has an opening through which you slide your hand and wrist. The cuff is wide, which gives it an innate feeling of supremacy. You might have to stack a number of bangles to make a statement, but one cuff worn as a wristband is plenty.

Early wrist cuffs would have served as portable protection and comfort in the face of the great unknown as humans ventured into the wider world. Possibly, they were important in socializing and making connections; wearing similar cuffs would have strengthened the bonds of community. The surfaces are wide to enable goldsmiths to practise engraving, hammering and tulle techniques on the wrist ornament. Although, due to their shape, they appear as cuffs which sit at the termination of a sleeve, their history predates shirt design. It wasn't until the 1500s that small ruffles – the ancestors of shirt cuffs – began to appear at wristbands.

The word 'cuff' comes from the Middle English *cuffe*, which meant 'glove' or 'mitten'. It is also used as a surname, which indicates that it might have originally been the occupational name of a glove maker. By the sixteenth century, a cuff generally meant a band around the base of a sleeve. Shirts had begun to expand beyond the boundaries of dresses, doublets and bodices and spilled out of sleeves over the wrist. They were embroidered with silk or metallic threads, pleated in complex shapes or ruffled as canvases illustrating a variety of linen or lace decorative effects. In time they were made to detach, so they could be easily cleaned and worn separately from the shirt. It would have required a small adjustment for these cuffs to be turned into an accessory made in a stronger material such as leather or metal. From a design point of view, the wide cuff made a convenient blank canvas for the artistic expression of the goldsmith, just as the linen cuff had been for the seamstress.

Whilst never losing its place on our wrists, the cuff has changed as it has journeyed with us through history, from commanding military ornaments, emotive family traditions and iconic jewels to minimalist fashion accessories. Cuffs exemplify common threads, shared cultures, traditions and fashions that tell stories through the ages.

LEATHER CUFFS

Leather clothing, and therefore I believe cuffs, emerged from Africa. It's often theorized that many human cognitive and evolutionary leaps were born from an 'adapt or die' mentality, but as early humans began to travel, they also took elements of style along with them for others to emulate. From the Middle Stone Age era, when humans were hunter-gatherers living in caves or simple huts, they used animal skins as clothing to provide warmth and protection from the weather, as well as safeguarding their feet from stones and thorns. Some of the oldest archaeological evidence of human clothing comes from a leather and fur production site that is 120,000 years old. The appearance of shells that had no nutritional benefit found alongside this leather apparel leads historians to believe they were valued for ornamentation purposes, which means prehistoric clothing could have been about style as well as functionality, in common with our own.

Emily Hallett, of the Max Planck Institute for the Science of Human History in Germany, was initially interested in the diet of Pleistocene humans, examining bones to see which animals were eaten and how they were butchered. Whilst excavating Contrebandiers Cave on Morocco's Atlantic Coast, however, she found dozens of shaped and polished bone tools, which would have been ideal for scraping hides and pelts clean to make leather and fur clothing. Nearby lay carnivore bones, which bore signs of having been cut by humans. The remains of wild cats and golden jackals showed similar marks to those used in skinning techniques today; incisions were made to detach the skin at each end of the animals' paws so that the skin could be pulled in one piece to the head.

The evidence suggests that North African cave dwellers were making and wearing clothing long before the great migrations of humans to which all living non-Africans can trace their roots. When *Homo sapiens* left Africa to populate the globe, it appears likely they may have been adorned by animal skins. Their knowledge of hunting and killing dangerous predators, skills in crafting and using specialized tools and labour as well as techniques of fur and leather processing would have journeyed with them.

'Clothing and the expanded toolkits of early humans are likely parts of the package that led to the adaptive success of humans,' Hallett says, 'and helped our ability to succeed globally and in climatically extreme regions.'

Blombos Cave in South Africa didn't only reveal bead ornamentation; there was also early evidence for clothing discovered. Scientists found stone cutting and scraping tools with bone awls, a pointed tool for making holes in leather, with microwear on the tips suggesting they were used to sew garments. Some much older sites have tools that suggest humans could have worn clothes hundreds of thousands of years ago, but the evidence is far less certain. By then, leather could have been fashioned into arm protectors.

We have the ancient Greeks to thank for the development of tanning formulas using certain barks and leaves to soften and preserve leather. This was the first record of vegetable-tanned leather, which interestingly is exactly what modern designers incorporating leather into bags, shoes and jewellery are returning to. It seems likely they might have discovered the process from leaving animal skins on wet forest ground, where the chemicals released by decaying leaves and vegetation would have naturally tanned them.

The Greeks were great admirers of leather's durable properties. Wide leather wristbands functioned as 'armour' and were part of the standard dress for armed conflict. Men of ancient Greece proudly brandished wristbands as a traditional part of their military uniform, a practice that was later adopted by the Celts and Romans.

During the Roman period, leather 'bracers' were worn by archers to protect their forearm from whiplash whilst shooting an arrow and prevented a loose sleeve from catching the bowstring. Sometimes a cuff was also worn to signify a particular soldier had shown bravery in battle and may also have been a leather interpretation of the *armilla*, an armband awarded as a military decoration to soldiers of ancient Rome for gallantry and valour. These were made in the form of a solid gold, open-sided cuff with a hinge, often decorated with legionary emblems and patterned, they took on the symbolic role of a war trophy.

Hollywood films such as *Hannibal*, *Quo Vadis* and *Cleopatra* are partly responsible for the enduring popular image of soldiers from the ancient world wearing leather cuffs. Costume designers will often use leather cuffs as part of a character's military costume as a fast-track way to symbolize strength, conjuring up the idea of muscle and power.

The notion of military might, and a certain type of bravery, has lingered in the perception of a leather cuff, and they have retained a slightly intimidating aura, perfect for people who wanted to stand out and command attention. Back in the day, no self-respecting rock star would be without a leather jacket and cuff – Keith Richards, Ozzy Osbourne and Alice Cooper amongst them. Leather was the androgynous uniform of the 1970s, and these non-traditional wristbands were indicative of a badass rock 'n' roll lifestyle. Nowadays I notice that, since the #MeToo movement, men have moved away from the tough-cuff leather look and are wearing more feminine beaded bracelets. Or else leather pieces, such as those designed by emerging jeweller Louie Cresswell, are softened with a sophisticated and luxurious diamond finish.

Meanwhile, Hollywood has remained faithful to the premise that going into battle requires cuffs. The difference is that, now more than ever, they are strapped to the wrists of females – superheroes such as Wonder Woman and Captain Marvel – as opposed to male soldiers. They remain the go-to symbol of strength, capable of repelling new age attacks such as 'omega beams' and 'heat vision' in the DC Universe. During the '70s, the comic book superhero Wonder Woman was depicted by actress Lynda Carter repelling bullets in each episode and creating a defensive forcefield when her cuffs clashed together. In 2020, Carter revealed she still owned her Wonder Woman cuffs, in part because 'wearing them still makes me feel like a total badass'.

In the modern world, cuffs equal protection and empowerment. Captain Marvel, the main character in the company's first female-led film, sports a metallic pair that glow with her unearthly energy. Brunnhilde, the fighting Valkyrie played by Tessa Thompson in *Thor*, is able to control the weapons of her gunship remotely using her leather and chainmail set. Meanwhile, in *Black Panther*, the ferocious Dora Milaje, the elite group of female bodyguards that are part of the Wakanda special forces, are adorned with matching cuffs by the jewellery designer Douriean Fletcher. The cuffs are intended to be imposing, serving as part protective body armour and part eye-catching ornament. The idea is that women harness the potential of cuffs to feel empowered.

William Moulton Marston, who invented the character of Wonder Woman in 1941, reported that the cuffs were based on the silver bracelets worn by his lover, Olive Byrne. Marston stated that Wonder Woman's cuffs were there to serve as a constant reminder of what happens to a girl when she lets a man rule her, as the Greeks once did the Amazons. It's a curious twist for the cuff that this traditionally male symbol of strength has been essentially co-opted by women to uphold and represent their author-ity – the physical embodiment of the new, post-#MeToo balance of power between the sexes.

The leather cuff made a fashion return in 2002 when the first De Beers diamond store opened on London's Bond Street. One of artistic director Reema Pachachi's new designs garnered particular attention: a leather wrist-let cuff studded with a diamond. Pachachi wanted to strip diamond jewellery of its stuffy, precious image and make it more youthful and easier to wear. The inspiration for the cuff came from the African origins of the brand and their muse, the supermodel Iman, and the idea was that you wore one on each arm.

The ultimate modern armour jewel was created by British jeweller Shaun Leane for style icon and musician

Daphne Guinness. Given the Latin name 'Contra Mundum', meaning 'against the world', the extraordinary diamond mesh-encrusted couture glove was intended to be a defence piece for the shy Guinness to wear. 'Shaun, Alexander McQueen and I were in the corner of the V&A Museum at one of those fashion things,' recalls Guinness. 'We were all just trying to hide in the corner and not be spoken to. So, I said, "Let's go and have a look at the armour".' That led to the idea of collaborating on an armoured glove. Shaun arrived at her house the following morning with a bucket in which to take a cast of her arm. In the end, it took twenty-one fittings and over four years to create the chainmail featuring 5,000 black and white diamonds, with each knuckle custom-fitting the fingertips. The piece was bought in 2020 by Lady Gaga.

Dog collars

Travel was instrumental in the creation of a new style of leather cuff crafted by artisans at Hermès, hunched over worktables hand-stitching vegetable-tanned cowhide in much the same way as the ancients. Thierry Hermès opened a workshop in Paris fashioning made-to-measure leather harnesses and saddles for clients looking for finesse as well as endurance in all conditions, and his work spread throughout Europe. One client requested a similarly worked dog collar for her beloved bulldog featuring a centre ring for a leash and decorative pyramid studs. By the mid-nineteenth century, every woman in Paris wanted one for her precious pooch. In time, dog owners and pets flaunted matching leather accessories when the Collier de Chien was adapted into a cuff – including the hoop for a lead, suggesting a role reversal.

JADE CUFFS

Called the 'stone of heaven', jade is prized above all others in China. Long been thought to have magical powers, the green stone is rich with moral and spiritual meaning. Indeed, its luminosity and ability to warm to the touch must have made it seem heaven-sent when it was first discovered in rocks washed down from the mountains in Central Asia.

Jade is actually a general term for two substances: nephrite and jadeite. Nephrite, which is durable and looks opaque, which the Chinese call 'mutton fat', has been used since prehistoric times to create objects from utensils to weapons. Jadeite is the more valuable stone, which has a beguiling green translucent appearance and is more commonly used for jewellery.

Jade is hard on the Mohs scale, tougher than steel, so direct carving with the rudimentary tools available at the time was impossible. Slow abrasion, using a cord and sand, was the only way to shape and manipulate the stone, which took time and patience. The effort required to shape the stone was compared to the discipline needed to train the mind, and this characteristic formed part of its emblematic profile, as well as heightening its value.

Confucius attributed human virtues to the stone, such as integrity, purity and fortitude. In the Han dynasty from 206 BCE to CE 220, it was believed to have vivifying properties. Emperors were buried in suits of jade to ensure immortality – indeed, in Chinese writing the character for jade is virtually the same as that used for emperor. Originally jade was used for intricate carvings, decorations, the finest statues and jewellery for wealthy and imperial families.

Its beauty and otherworldly qualities are so potent that the belief in the stone's influence endures. Even today Chinese businesspeople like to hold or wear jade during an important meeting, to protect their interests. People often wear a jade bracelet, believing that jade should always be nearby because, when handled, something of the stone's secret virtue is absorbed into the body. To give some idea of the importance of jade in China, when I visited one of the Chow Tai Fook jewellery stores in Hong Kong, of which there were sixteen outlets on one long street, I witnessed a near constant stream of people who came in to weigh their gold and often exchange it for jade bangles. To the Chinese, gold is valuable. As a cultural, aesthetic and financial investment, however, it cannot compare to jade, which is invaluable. Inside the translucent stone shines the green light associated with

Asian history, cultural ties and heritage. It is an emblem that links them to their ancestors.

Traditionally, older Chinese and Vietnamese women wear jadeite around their wrists as a life-giving force to protect and heal the body and to ward off bad spirits. Mostly they hope to pass the jewel down to the next generation, who will carry the weight of the family history on their wrist, symbolizing unbreakable bonds across the generational divide. For many Asian American girls, wearing a jade cuff tethers them to their homeland and heritage. The green colour also evokes the snow-capped mountain landscape of fertile rolling hills and deep river valleys.

Some young people, who may have viewed their grandmothers' or aunts' bangles as old-fashioned and out of date in their teens, are now discovering the culture and pushing designers to be more experimental in their use of jade. New colour options are being explored such as lavender, yellow, red and even black, which is in fact deep green with a high iron content, as well as an 'icy' shade of jade fused with crystals. These cuffs are meshing their Asian heritage seamlessly with Westernized lifestyles.

Jadeite remains the most sought-after colour, however, and comes with astonishing price tags. Even modest-looking bangles can be priced over $100,000. When I visited, Chow Tai Fook had acquired a rare 350g jadeite stone valued at HK $100 million (£10 million) and a jade necklace that once belonged to the American heiress Barbara Hutton was sold by Sotheby's Hong Kong for a record-breaking US$27.44 million.

In December 2022, the London-based brand Asprey announced, in partnership with Oxford University, an exclusive collection of imperial jadeite jewellery pieces, having developed a technology to improve certification standards of the stone. One jadeite bangle, inspired by the art deco pieces in their archive, is fitted with a diamond hinge and clasp so it's easily opened and the wearer doesn't have to squeeze their hand through the centre.

The Covid pandemic accelerated opportunities for digital platforms and a form of distanced trading, so today, there's no need to travel to acquire a jade cuff. The Chinese culture can enter your home via state-of-the-art video technology, enabling easy close inspection of the gemstone. These will no doubt be a beautiful and wearable stone of value, but without the heirloom factor. It's the art of travel, albeit the small movement of passing the solid seamless piece of green stone from wrist to wrist, that recalls the traditions that help define people; traditions that remind them where they come from.

IVORY CUFFS

From the sixteenth century, the Kingdom of Benin produced the most intricate and beautifully worked ivory cuffs. Ivory was traded for hundreds of years in Africa and Asia and human lust for ivory tusks led to a frenzy of slaughter that reduced the elephant population from 26 million in 1800 to around 450,000 today. In 1989, there was a worldwide ban on ivory sales but unfortunately an illegal trade continues, and behind every piece of ivory jewellery and trinket lies a dead elephant. Indeed, I've often been asked whether a person, having inherited an antique ivory jewel, should wear it at all. My feeling is that ivory should exist now only in museums as relics of a bygone age.

Mammoth ivory provides a modern, cruelty-free alternative to elephant ivory for jewellers, but this can come with its own issues of environmental damage. This type of ivory is found in Siberia during the summer months, when the tundra melts, but to retrieve the tusks, a water pump is used, which can disturb the earth in the vicinity, risking a collapse or flood.

The ivory cuffs crafted in the Kingdom of Benin during the sixteenth century are now housed in institutions like the British Museum and New York's Metropolitan Museum of Art. The artists who created the inlaid armlets were inspired from abroad. The kingdom's craftsmen and guilds were in contact with sea traders and crewmen who made regular journeys to India, Ceylon, Japan and China, and it is not surprising that delicate carved cuffs found in Benin City showed Asian influence as well as techniques used by Renaissance goldsmiths. The Oba wore pairs of ornate cylindrical ivory cuffs, deploying iconography that reinforced his divine authority. The brass structures were inlaid with elephant ivory, a material which was associated with ritual purity and the spirit world.

These cuffs, like the Greek leather cuffs, were symbols of power and strength. Ivory carvers worked exclusively for the state to glorify religious and political order, and their intricate carvings illustrate the Oba's role as king, the history of Benin and the belief system of the Edo people. The ivory cuffs would be worn in ceremonies. One depicts the Oba wielding a ceremonial sword, showing his control of Benin's military. Another cuff depicts the Oba holding crocodiles up towards the sky, which was believed to link him with the god Olokun, the ruler of the sea.

The Benin artisans refined the lost-wax technique, a method of casting brass in which a molten metal is poured into a mould, created by means of a wax model, until they were able to cast plaques only an eighth of an inch thick, in an artistic technique that was practised by Renaissance 'masters' in Europe which must have travelled with traders visiting the kingdom. The richly decorated detail might depict the Oba carved in the centre wearing an elaborate crown and beaded band across his chest, raising an *eben* (sword) in one hand and with his other firmly holding the forearm of one of his warriors, expressing his control of Benin's military might. Portuguese soldiers would be flanking them, a reference to their role as Benin's military partners during the sixteenth century, surrounded by decorative motifs including crocodiles and mudfish.

The production of works of art was organized amongst various guilds in Benin, and throughout much of its history, the use of ivory was restricted. Anyone who wished to commission Igbesanmwan, the royal guild for ivory carvers, had to place their request through the Oba. The success of Benin was fuelled by its lively trading relationships with Europeans, who sought the kingdom's artwork, gold, ivory and pepper. During the 1700s, the restriction on the use of ivory was relaxed, and the Dutch began to fulfil the European demand for ivory. Elephant hunting was intensified, and firearms increased the efficiency of the hunters as thousands of tusks were exported to Europe each year. Some were retained for Benin artists from which to carve altar tusks, cuffs and masks as well as containers, ornaments and salt cellars, all of which were prized by European traders.

When the British tried to expand their own trade in the nineteenth century, the Benin people killed their envoys. In 1897, the British sent an armed expedition to destroy the Oba's palace and take away large quantities of sculpture and regalia, including works in wood, ivory and brass. The British Museum has had an audience with His Royal Majesty Oba Ewuare II, who has requested for Benin collections to be returned to the country, and discussions continue with Nigeria's National Commission for Museums and Monuments about the opportunity of sharing and displaying objects from the Kingdom of Benin.

The craft of the lost-wax technique continues in African-inspired cuffs. Ivory no longer features; stones are sustainably sourced from African gem cutters using stones from Mozambique, Kenya and Zambia combined with the gold heritage of Africa. Ghanaian-born jewellery designer-maker Emefa Cole, has returned to the roots of her homeland. Ashanti was the centre of the regional gold trade accumulating wealth and glory during the seventeenth and eighteenth centuries. Cole is learning the lost-wax technique from the personal goldsmiths of the Asantehene in Kumasi, the King of Ashanti's jewellers, who perfected the art. The heritage of artistry as well as the drama of the colours, textures and tones of the African landscape are explored in her work. The Vulcan cuff explodes with seeming liquid metal echoing the flow of molten rock and magma in motion, whilst sculptural textured surfaces of the Igneous cuff chime with the idea of erosion. She only uses Single Mine Origin gold with a QR code tracing the precise journey and hands through which the gold has passed on its way from the mine to the cuff. Whilst as bold and fearless as the Benin cuffs, these jewels shine with a new African story for the modern era, changing the historic narrative of a continent plundered for its riches. Rather these cuffs distil the cultural heritage and artistry of Africa into contemporary pieces. Cole is intrigued by geology, the constant changes to our world and the precious materials which might remain buried if not for erosion or mining. And yet the cuffs aren't solely symbolic of nature's renewal, they also depict a new African story of understated luxury whilst maintaining the tradition of goldsmithing. African jewellers don't replicate the Benin or Ashanti cuff techniques, the idea is to use them with modern ways of working to create something new. Cole is now a guardian of the precious and time-honoured Ashanti secrets, ready to pass the knowledge onto a new generation of metalsmiths.

Glass cuffs

Two historic events during the late eighteenth and early nineteenth centuries significantly changed the style of the cuff. Firstly, new discoveries made in the ruins of the ancient Roman cities of Pompeii and Herculaneum were reflected in wide cuffs adorned with complex glass mosaic scenes of classical motifs, including decoratively engraved golden ears of wheat, honeysuckle, palmette, laurel and blue enamel Greek key patterns. The second event which sparked an interest in glass cuffs was the defeat of Napoleon, which made travel throughout Europe possible again. Visitors, including aristocratic young men on their 'Grand Tour', travelled to France, Italy and Switzerland to complete their cultural and artistic education. Whilst Venice is often considered the centre of Italy's glass manufacture, Rome is responsible for one of the country's most distinguished art forms: micro mosaics.

Intricate mosaic jewels, a speciality of Italian

workshops, captured the beautiful scenery of the Italian countryside and other typical Italianate scenes, such as Roman ruins and religious iconography, comprised of tiny tesserae of coloured glass. These micro mosaics were made using ancient methods of glass paste spinning, a long and meticulous process during which glass paste is heated over a flame and 'hand-spun' and pulled into rods or threads. The rods are allowed to cool and solidify before being split by hand, one by one, into minuscule cubed tiles, or tesserae. The workshops boasted a rainbow colour library of thousands of shades with matte or shiny surfaces.

A Roman craftsman would use pointed tweezers to arrange hundreds of the rectangular tesserae, each tiny tile less than one millimetre wide, in mastic or cement on a glass panel to assemble a perfectly rendered scene. These miniature works of art could be compared to impressionism in the way that the finished work resembled a painting but moving closer one could see outlines of the tiles. It's possible to gauge how popular these micro-mosaic panels were by the fact that there were 150–200 workshops in Rome alone by the mid-nineteenth century creating mosaics.

Fashionable women during the nineteenth century as well as 'Grand Tourists' made their way to the shop of Fortunato Pio Castellani by the Trevi fountain, who had initiated a new archaeological revival style emulating Roman and Etruscan techniques. The glass micro mosaics were influenced by classical antiquity and early Christian and Byzantine church mosaics taking the form of religious iconography, Latin and Greek inscriptions as well as pastoral scenes, birds and insects. Castellani had been granted special permission by the Vatican specifically to view previously unseen objects in the Regolini-Galassi tomb and from studying these he began to use a combination of ancient techniques to mimic the look of antique gold. The glass micro mosaics would be centrally set into wide cuffs displaying granulation, a process by which small gold grains were meticulously fixed onto the surface of the metal bracelet.

The city of Florence specialized in *pietra dura*, or hardstone mosaics. Some cuffs featured micro mosaic inlays, precisely cut and fitted together to form a puzzle-like picture using malachite, lapis lazuli, aventurine and turquoise. The scenes depicted were Italian sites, landscapes, classical mythology and vistas, sometimes with coral accents, garnets or shell. These cuffs were proudly worn home as the latest fashion, with the bonus of conferring on the wearer an appreciation of classical history.

Tourists to Naples, within the shadow of Mount Etna, purchased jewellery carved from coral, tortoiseshell and an earthy-coloured 'lava' limestone, particularly in carved cameos, a method of carving with a raised image in relief. Ancient and Renaissance types of carving were practised mainly with stones like onyx and agate with integral layers to produce the effect of a portrait or scene against a contrasting coloured background.

The discoveries in Pompeii and Herculaneum sparked

a new fashion for engraved gems which were rare and expensive. A Scottish gem engraver and modeller James Tassie determined to make glass cameos to meet this new demand which were less expensive and could be mass-produced. He invented a secret formula in opaque and transparent glass forms to replicate any colour or pattern of a precious gemstone. When the paste had a soft consistency, it could take impressions in a moulding process featuring Roman and Greek symbolism from classical antiquity, replicating a classical cameo, but the open back setting allowed light to flood through each 'tassie' so it shone like a precious stone. Often several were mounted on gold links forming two rows creating a wide cuff style. These travelled around the world even captivating Catherine the Great, who commissioned a collection of Tassie's gem imitations.

Interestingly, many gemstones used in cuffs and other jewels at the time were mounted with a closed back dimming their colours. The use of tinted and silvered copper sheets to 'foil' the gems became standard practice to brighten diamonds and intensify coloured stones. No foil was necessary for 'tassies' but often the vibrant glass cuffs and beaded bracelets created in Venice gleamed with gold and silver threads embedded within the liquid glass.

The craft of glassmaking involves melting mineral sands at temperatures between 1,700–2,700 degrees Fahrenheit into flexible liquid glass, before being removed from the furnace and shaped using various specialized instruments and hand decorated by the artisan under a heat lamp. Glass makers were mainly producing Rosetta glass bead bracelets made by layering glass in various colours in a mould. But by the nineteenth century they had rediscovered the complex and ancient millefiori technique characterized by dense psychedelic floral patterns. Glass canes are produced called murrine, a cylinder created by soft glass in colours stacked on top of one another. Multicoloured threads, metal leaf and aventurine can be inserted into soft glass to create patterns embedded in the canes, which are then sliced in a cross section to resemble a thousand flowers, stars or birds. Now they sparkle in candy colours on young girls' wrists, unaware their fashionable new cuff is inspired by the centuries-old aesthetic. The shift towards handmade has pushed designers to include glass elements in jewellery, including cuffs and bracelets.

Dolce & Gabbana work with craftsmen using one of the last existing historical furnaces in the city. The iconography of the miniature mosaics chime with the golden figures and floral elements depicted on the Byzantine art and mosaics covering the walls, vaults and dome of the Basilica of St Mark's. Different perspectives of Venice are rendered as miniature artworks, echoing the cityscapes by Italian painter Canaletto, featuring views across the lagoon, honey-gold palazzos that line the Grand Canal and the city's two most famous bridges, the Rialto and the Bridge of Sighs, in which the lustrous glass tiles reflect the white Istrian stone bridges shining in the water below. These jewels in the tradition of eighteenth-century portable artworks are carried home as mementoes and keepsakes of the dappled columns, stone arches and palazzos of an Italian journey. You can still find nineteenth-century 'souvenir' bracelets on antique sites whose gold rectangles unfold to spell Roma or gleam with mosaic snapshots of a historic building or vista. Castellani blue micro mosaics also conveyed the word Roma, making the quintessential souvenir for those enamoured of their visit, as the intention was to read Amor in reverse. These glass cuffs express Italy's artistic customs in miniature and glint from wrists as cultural artefacts.

Diamond cuffs

Hollywood became the centre of design and fashion during the 1920s. News reels and magazines paraded movie stars and the treasures from their own jewel boxes, and every city had a department store for women to buy similar costume pieces and participate in that fantasy. If you watched actresses with stacks of cuffs and bracelets, you could aspire to own costume versions. Paris still led couture dressing, but Hollywood was more universal and women everywhere wanted to emulate the sultry stars of the silver screen.

Even before the phrase 'diamonds are a girl's best friend' was uttered in *Gentlemen Prefer Blondes*, diamonds were synonymous with Hollywood. A star bedecked in diamonds broke through the illusion of film and brought fantasies to life, resonating with the dreams and imaginations of movie-goers. Actresses embodied audiences' expectations of on-screen luxurious coquetry, and diamond cuffs often laid over elbow-length satin gloves were a major part of that lavish look. The blonde not-so-dumb bombshell had also arrived in our consciousness, and in beauty parlours around the country women mimicked Jean Harlow's platinum look as well as her wrist crammed with diamond and gemstone art deco bracelets over a white satin glove.

In 1929, Mary Pickford received the Academy Award for best actress whilst wearing a wide diamond bracelet, satisfying the public's desire for glamour, with the added benefit of raising box office earnings of her film *Coquette*. Marlene Dietrich wore her own cabochon emerald and diamond bracelet in *Desire* and a massive ruby and diamond Mystery Set cuff by Van Cleef & Arpels in *Stage Fright*. Paulette Goddard's emerald cabochon and diamond floral cuff, seen on her arm in George Cukor's *The Women*, was a gift from her husband Charlie Chaplin and bought from one of the most popular jewellers in Hollywood, Trabert & Hoeffer-Mauboussin. In 1937, Paul Flato opened his jewellery store on Sunset Boulevard, and celebrities flocked to the store for his large-scale theatrical pieces. Merle Oberon wore a cache of Flato designs, including a cuff remarkably like her own polished gold bow, holding a 195-carat citrine, in the film *That Uncertain Feeling.*

The diamond cuffs Mae West wore both on and off screen were instrumental in her creation of her controversial sex-siren character 'Diamond Lil', which inspired a generation. And although she later sold most of her jewellery to donate funds to the war effort, she did keep a 40-carat diamond bracelet, which remained in her collection and is now in the archive collection of US-based jeweller Neil Lane. For special occasions he loans it to stars such as Madonna and Catherine Zeta-Jones to sparkle just like Diamond Lil.

If any American fictional character of the twentieth century seems likely to be immortal, it is Lorelei Lee of Little Rock, Arkansas, the not-so-dumb blonde who knew that diamonds are a girl's best friend. Outrageous, charming and unforgettable, she was portrayed by Marilyn Monroe in Howard Hawks's *Gentlemen Prefer Blondes* and has become the archetype of the footloose, good-hearted gold-digger with an insatiable appetite for diamonds. The jewels that appeared in the film over a pink satin glove were Swarovski crystal, created by Joseff of Hollywood for the film, but the narrative and luxurious coquetry of Monroe convinced audiences they were the real thing.

It's easy to reduce Lorelei to merely a gold-digger, but she is looking for power and access in a culture driven by money and knows that kissing a hand may make you feel good, but a diamond cuff makes a desirable pension plan which lasts forever. Few other cinematic performances have stood the test of time like Monroe singing 'Diamonds are a Girl's Best Friend', which has become something of a legend. The song is often understood as a celebration of materialism, but it's really about a woman's desire for financial independence during an age when that was difficult to achieve. The song constructed an idea of femininity as women moved towards a modern expression of greater freedom. Her pink-gloved look overlaid with diamond cuffs has been mimicked ever since by celebrities such as Madonna, Kylie Minogue, Geri Halliwell and many more.

A diamond cuff over a glove remains alluring to this day, and Dua Lipa recently updated the look at the Grammys with wide diamonds over black latex. One hundred years later, our fascination with art deco cuffs is more intense than ever.

The cuff was and still remains the jewel for a generation of independent women looking for something empowering and unassailably glamorous. Cuffs are armour-like, yet sensual and sophisticated, to be worn conspicuously. Socialite and style icon Daisy Fellowes followed the cuff trend and turned heads in 1926 when she wore manchette diamond-patterned wide cuffs offset with fringes of emerald drops. Wearing pairs of bracelets became her signature style, described by Cecil Beaton as 'studied simplicity'. Inspired by Indian Mughal designs, they came as a matching pair, which, she explained, she wore 'for balance'.

MALTESE CUFFS

The legendary Parisian designer Coco Chanel once said: 'The point of jewellery isn't to make a woman look rich but to adorn her; not the same thing.' When *Vogue* published her design of a simple black crêpe de Chine dress in 1926, with long narrow sleeves and accessorized with a single strand of white pearls, she changed fashion forever. It was simple and accessible to women of all classes, and *Vogue* rightly predicted 'it would become a sort of uniform for all women of taste.' When Chanel appeared wearing white beach pyjamas with jewelled cuffs on Venice's Lido, white was immediately 'in vogue'.

Chanel had an impressive roster of lovers and suitors from whom she received a treasury of precious pearls and gems. The Duke of Westminster allegedly gave her a jewel every week with a bouquet of flowers and the Grand Duke Dmitri Pavlovich also showered her with fine jewels. Unfortunately, it was jewellery that didn't suit her style.

During the 1930s, Chanel was introduced to Fulco Santostefano della Cerda, the Duke of Verdura, a Sicilian nobleman who'd travelled to Paris with aspirations to be an artist. He began designing textiles for Chanel before she asked him to take apart the valuable antiques given to her by her titled lovers and create something that she would wear – that would represent emancipation for women in the same way that her fashion was currently freeing women from corsets and lace frills, offering them sailor shirts and wide-leg pants instead. Her clothes were androgynous and fluid; she wanted women to move and breathe in their clothes in the same way that men did. She wanted a new style of jewel to similarly free women from wearing what she considered vulgar displays of wealth around their necks and wrists.

Verdura's inspiration for the iconic cuffs he was to create for Chanel came from travelling and absorbing other cultures. The two of them visited museums around Europe studying the Renaissance jewels at the Treasury of Munich as well as the collection of Augustus the Strong and Charlemagne in Dresden. They vacationed in Italy transfixed by the glittering Byzantine mosaic murals of Empress Theodora in Ravenna's Basilica di San Vitale.

Following this trip, the design he fashioned adapted the Maltese cross – sometimes referred to as the Amalfi – to decorate broad enamel cuffs. Within the golden outline of the cross, he placed a Byzantine-like mosaic collection of semi-precious gems arranged in a seemingly haphazard design of different sizes and colours.

The Maltese cross is a symmetrical, eight-pointed symbol composed of four arrowheads, which was adopted by a group of Christian warriors called the Order of the Knights of St John. Established in 1048, they cared for the sick and injured in the Holy Land and from 1530 ruled the Maltese islands for over two centuries. The knights put their stamp on these islands through architecture and patronage of the arts, and the Maltese cross was used on coats of arms, palaces, fortifications, churches and monuments as well as frescoes and smaller-scale coins, silverware and jewellery.

The idea for the cross could have evolved from viewing the Ravenna mosaics, or Verdura's childhood in Palermo, not far from the Amalfi coast and the island of Malta. It was a jewelled interpretation of the star of the Knights of Malta aesthetic he would have absorbed – consciously or not – when he was growing up.

The cuffs blurred the lines between fine and costume jewels, and Chanel was pictured constantly wearing them as a pair, one on each wrist. Always the trendsetter, a host of fashionable independent women soon followed suit, including Diana Vreeland, Nancy Cunard, Millicent Rogers and Helena Rubinstein. The style was about taste, not tradition.

Chanel was the first designer to make costume jewellery a key element of her shows, collaborating with Parisian jeweller Robert Goossens to create costume versions of the Maltese cuffs and other Byzantine and baroque styles for the runway. She presented Goossens with hefty volumes of antique jewellery to serve as inspiration and it is not an overstatement to say she duly changed the course of women's fashion. The landscape of the accessory world changed; costume jewels became not only acceptable, but chic.

Chanel's minimalist fashion was the perfect canvas for the opulent couture jewellery she created with Goossens. 'When you make something fake', she explained at the time, 'it's always on a bigger scale.' The collaboration began in 1954 and is still going strong today. Maison Goossens is one of the few ateliers specializing in Chanel's Métier d'art of traditional decorative techniques created by artisans, making costume jewellery, buttons and belt buckles for the French fashion house.

Maltese cuffs continue to be worn by contemporary style icons such as Sarah Jessica Parker, Brooke Shields and Sofia Coppola. The cuffs embodied the manner in which Chanel wore all her gems – precious or otherwise. Like sparkling time-travellers, they retained the spirit of ancient jewels, rather than the precise form of the original. It was a stylistic revolution bringing what had been an ancient ethos into the modern era.

SCANDINAVIAN SILVER CUFF

Danish silversmith Vivianna Torun Bülow-Hübe, born in 1927, was another early feminist and ground-breaking woman who strove to disassociate jewellery from being objects of high wealth, status and value. 'I was thinking about the type of woman who went around in mink coats and extravagant jewellery,' she said, 'which they kept in safes for fear of theft, showing off how much their husbands were worth, or just how much they were worth to their husbands. To me, this was horrendous. I thought women should be independent and go out to work.'

A true pioneer in every sense of the word, Torun

Bülow-Hübe began an altogether different style of simple silver jewellery with a purity of form and took cuffs in the opposite direction of the 'diamonds are a girl's best friend' look.

Her jewellery is essentially an interpretation of nature, made using steel, silver rutilated quartz and beach pebbles. She loved organic forms like leaves, pools and spirals, and her pieces flow with a sensuous life of their own which shines defiantly years later with an eternal modernity. Spiralling silver jewels and cuffs seem so alive and expressive. She lived in many different countries throughout her life and spoke six languages, so was influenced by other cultures. Plus, of course, as a Scandinavian, there are aspects of her own culture and heritage in the round Viking-esque purity and simplicity of silver torques swinging with a quartz stone or a pebble she collected beachcombing with Picasso in the South of France.

Something she really disliked was the relentlessness of time, and that's why she made a wide silver spoon-shaped cuff watch, which was open on the side. The face was blank, stripped of numbers, reflecting the wearer's image back like a mirror, urging you to be introspective and not feel the pressure of time. She added only hands to count seconds, a reminder that we should live in the now – every second now – and this was in 1969, decades ahead of the popular psychology tropes that began to urge us all to live in the moment.

She preferred working with silver for its softness on the

skin and lack of pretension, and for her, pebbles washed up on the beach, polished by the sea for hundreds of years, made the most beautiful alternative to precious stones.

Above all, she wanted her jewellery to give young women self-esteem, to reflect the woman and draw attention to her value in her own right.

Bone cuff

During the 1970s an Italian ex-model Elsa Peretti, who'd studied interior design, created a new style of jewellery for women which became a part of design history. Responding to working women, she designed jewellery they could buy for themselves and wear from day to night for their own pleasure. Her barrier-breaking diamonds by the yard were affordable for all women, and at the beginning these free-flowing diamond-dotted chains were sold for as little as $85. It was an important message for women at the time: you don't need a man to buy you jewellery.

Peretti was a visionary with an instinct for minimalism, using silver, jade and rock crystal in pure organic forms, and arguably had the greatest impact on fashion of any jeweller of the twentieth century. She arrived at Tiffany's with a unique sense of glamour, pioneering a new style and introducing a cuff that turned the tide of jewellery design forever.

When she first arrived in New York from Barcelona, where she'd been sitting for Salvador Dalí, she was a regular on the city's Studio 54 party scene, becoming a friend to Halston, the leading 1970s New York designer, and darling of such greats of fashion photography as Helmut Newton and Francesco Scavullo. Her first design was made for fashion designer Giorgio Sant'Angelo: a sterling silver bud vase worn around the neck on a leather thong, in which a rose with its stem wrapped in dampened tissue could live for several hours.

It was Halston's suggestion that she designed jewellery for his fashion collection, later introducing her to Walter Hoving, the legendary chairman of Tiffany & Co., who only needed to see one hand-carved coral bud vase and a silver cuff bracelet before signing her exclusively to Tiffany as a named designer.

Growing up in Rome, Peretti often walked down to the bottom of the Via Veneto to the Church of Santa Maria della Concezione dei Cappuccini. She recounted trembling with fear and excitement as she walked down the steep marble steps to the five subterranean chapels below, whose walls were encrusted with the bones of 9,000 Capuchin monks. One day she took a bone home with her because she liked the way it felt, knotty and smooth. Her mother was furious, sending her back to the chapel to return it. Later, she was struck upon arriving in Barcelona by the Casa Batlló, designed by Antoni Gaudí, with its facade that appears as if it's been made from skulls and bones. The skulls are the balconies, with the bones as support-ing pillars.

These experiences inspired her ground-breaking

sculptural bone cuff design, which appears to be moulded around the wrist bone. The only way Peretti could judge the design was to wear the piece for a few days. 'It has to go with the body, not against it,' she said. 'First it must feel good, then it must look good.' Sculptural, organic-looking and sensuous were all words that describe the cuff shaped around the knotty turns and curves of the wrist. Despite working with Halston, Peretti was adamant that jewellery wasn't fashion – her pieces were more like objects that became parts of the body.

Societal changes were taking place at the time, and working women saw Peretti's diamonds by the yard and bone cuff as reflective of their generation and the ongoing women's movement. A fellow star of '70s fashion, designer Diane Von Furstenberg, who created the wrap dress, said of Peretti: 'She was the one who brought a totally new concept into the jewellery field, making things you want to touch and hold'. The instant success of the cuff sparked *Newsweek* to announce it as jewellery's 'new dazzle', describing Peretti's work as 'the most revolutionary changes in serious jewellery since the Renaissance.'

Half a century later, her timeless cuff design has transcended fashion and endures across generations, remaining a modern-looking bestseller. Indeed, it was seen recently at the Academy Awards on the wrists of Liza Minelli, Venus Williams and Hailey Bieber, on the same night.

HANDCUFFS

Amongst all the freedom, liberation and free love during the 1970s, there was one cuff clicking onto women's wrists which made them captive: the Cartier Love Bracelet.

A wedding ring might be worn for better or worse – but in bad times, could be easily removed. The feelings demonstrated by a Love Bangle, however, weren't so easily cast asunder.

The bangle, designed by Aldo Cipullo, has a special locking mechanism that makes it impossible to remove without a tiny golden screwdriver. The turner of the screw is, in effect, the keeper of their lover's heart. Couples locked them symbolically onto each other's wrists, never to be removed, and they became a symbol of infinite love worn by such romantics as Elizabeth Taylor, Sophia Loren, Ali MacGraw, Steve McQueen, Cary Grant and Dyan Cannon.

They were minimal, modern and mechanistic, which was something totally new. Decades later these modern 'handcuffs' remain the most frequently googled piece of jewellery in the world. Some hospitals in New York keep a screwdriver handy because so many people come in 'cuffed' and medics need to be able to remove it quickly during an emergency.

History doesn't relate if those who wore a Love Bangle knew that their wrists were handcuffed by something that was inspired by the medieval chastity belt. Cipullo reportedly viewed the belt as an instrument of purity and loyalty and wanted to design a modern jewel that would represent a couple's fidelity and dependability, enforced or otherwise.

At the time, another jeweller was putting handcuffs on the fashion crowd. Parisian designer Dinh Van created gold *menottes*, which could also answer to the description of an ornamental shackle.

Van was born in 1927 in the Paris suburb of Boulogne-Billancourt to a French mother and a Vietnamese father who was a lacquer artist at Cartier. After studying drawing at the École Nationale Supérieure des Arts Décoratifs and metalwork, he apprenticed at Cartier and within a few years was producing high jewellery, such as a tiger-themed lorgnette commissioned by the Duchess of Windsor, under the direction of the artistic director of high jewellery, Jeanne Toussaint. But all the time he was drawn to contemporary fashion. It was the progressive clothes being designed for young women by Yves Saint Laurent, Pierre Cardin and Paco Rabanne, pioneering ready-to-wear fashion in Paris, the traditional home of couture, that inspired him. Geometric ensembles produced by *stylistes,* as they were then called, including Sonia Rykiel and Emmanuelle Khanh, and the early, modernist work of Emanuel Ungaro, were loosening the power of haute couture. Change was in motion. Fashion was taking youthful looks from boutique styles and the girl on the street, and Van was determined to create jewellery that chimed with the new atmosphere. He observed women on the streets and tried to reflect what they wore, calling his jewellery 'the mirror of life'.

His jewellery was about life today, with contemporary, clean-cut lines and a radical shimmery simplicity. He fashioned revolutionary-style military ID tags, razor blades and unisex cuffs decades before genderless jewellery was spoken about in fashion. The cuffs were inspired by a door key, featuring an angled motif designed to join and interlock. The centrepiece is the clasp, and the bracelet was named 'the handcuff' because, once closed, it's difficult to reopen. He was preoccupied with taking jewellery out of the safe and making it resonate with a new generation, creating a cuff with a rebellious, youthful spirit to recognize something as old as time: the union of two people.

ETHICAL CUFFS

As sustainability moves to the core of how we all aspire to live, new styles of cuffs are reflecting a code of transparency when it comes to the journeys of their stones and jewellery. Gen Z and millennial consumers in particular press for full environmental disclosure. Understanding where the stones originated is crucial, as are guarantees of safe practices and, of course, that there is no child labour involved. These generations would like to know down to the last penny that a fair wage was paid all the way along the supply chain, that healthcare and pensions should be in place and cutters of tiny stones scheduled for regular eye checks. Preferably, any gold used should be recycled or Fairmined. In years to come, these cuffs will reflect the twenty-first century's desire to track and trace every element within a piece of jewellery.

The most advanced blockchain-backed technologies and platforms are being used by brands, mining conglomerates and individual designers to enable traceability criteria to be met, as well as proof of provenance, and that healthy working conditions, sustainability targets and net-zero carbon emissions are all positively accounted for. De Beers is exploring how kimberlite, the rock encasing diamonds, can trap and store carbon emissions. It turns out that it has carbon-zapping powers, in which case mines could provide a sustainable solution for the luxury world as carbon-storage facilities.

Each cuff effectively needs a passport to prove that its evolution has been positive every step of the way. Ethical bodies are linking artisanal producers with social media so that everyone now has a voice and can reach foreign marketplaces to sell their work for fair prices. For instance, the premium paid for the sustainably sourced gold from the Cotapata Fairtrade gold mine in Bolivia is reinvested into local roads, schools and community projects. Some cuffs, which feature an organic gem formed from fossilized ammonite shells from the First Nation land in Alberta, Canada, benefit the local indigenous community.

The science and technology are vital, but they must be working in tandem with ancient jewellery traditions, skills and techniques to enable artisanal networks and individuals around the globe to survive economically. Plus, the complex enamelling and lacquering work carried out by local artisans in India and Afghanistan should be noted and credited.

Anthropologist Pippa Small is an eco-jeweller working closely with craftspeople in conflict areas around the globe to produce ethical cuffs. She works with the non-profit organization Turquoise Mountain to provide employment and encourage the survival of heritage skills, which in certain countries are fading arts. Turquoise Mountain ensures they are passed on and not lost, something considered to be an imperative by the charity's founders, King Charles III and the organization's president, Shoshana Stewart. Currently working in Myanmar, Afghanistan, Saudi Arabia and Jordan, Turquoise Mountain helps teach artisans traditional skills, in designs that will resonate globally, for economic survival. These skills will also enable women to live close to their communities. Crafts are often abandoned during turbulent times, but in this way the work produced acts as both an economic and cultural survival vehicle.

Recently, in Kabul, Small initiated the Zindagi Now programme, a legacy of Turquoise Mountain, which is run by female Afghans as a facility approved by the Taliban offering a one-year graduate programme in jewellery making, business and English. The students are bussed each day to the centre and provided with a hot meal at lunchtime. The girls hunch over workbenches as slim fingers nimbly twist golden wires like fine hair into the shape of a cuff, before polishing it with a 'ponytail' of cotton threads. However counter-intuitive it seems, jewellery has an important role to play during times of struggle and war.

Handcrafts and jewellery-making give these women a way to be seen and heard in the outside world, offering visibility and hope. The jewellery is also a way to preserve identities, both for individuals as well as in a wider cultural sense. The work offers distraction and boosts morale, as well as providing future employment and a local income stream. Every day there are digitally delivered design consultations, lectures and talks in the space available to any women who want to attend. As well as the offer of independence, the rhythmic ritual of hand working metal can become a part of a meditative healing process for lives torn apart by violence.

Vintage cuffs form part of a circular economy in jewellery, satisfying the modern demand for consuming less. The idea that cuffs are 'heirlooms' to be passed down the generations is taking hold in the Western world. Jewellers are not reacting to fast fashion seasons and trends. Cuffs are created with a timeless design and lifespan. A new age cuff gleams with more than their stylish appeal. There's a dedication in designers working to make sustainability and social benefit as important as the design. The cuffs can have a positive impact not only on your life but many others in distant places who may live in conflict in circumstances far removed from our own.

SUSTAINABLE CUFFS

This chapter ends where it began – with leather. Rather than animal hides, however, there are now sustainable leather alternatives for the eco-conscious buyer of a cuff.

Mycelium is produced from the root-like system of mushrooms and offers one alternative to animal hide, whilst other fermentation processes are used to grow animal-free collagen protein to assemble a material which is inspired by leather. There's even talk about a future 3D process which could grow a cuff and accessories as large as a Hermès Birkin bag.

Whilst humans still eat meat, however, there will be skin products that are wasted. Maria Sole Ferragamo is appealing to cool, young, eco-minded girls by upcycling leather, deftly engineering what would have otherwise been discarded into landfill. The leftover material is persuaded into sculptural shapes and origami-like textures in sparkling iridescent gold, silver and fuchsia, transformed into a soft fabric for wide cuffs that look as if they've been honed from precious metals.

Ferragamo is guided by the leftover materials she finds in the Italian shoe factories owned by her family. 'The value of working with leftover material is that there's always this sense of uniqueness,' she explains, 'given by nature of the availability of the material itself.' The materials often come with no information as to their origins – although she did find out later that by chance the first brass shavings she used with leather 'came from the clasp of a Ferragamo bag'.

Dramatic cuffs have also been created by designer Diane Kordas, using waste from the fishing and food industries, such as discarded salmon skins. In South Africa, ostrich skins are discarded as waste, and Kordas dyes these into colours using an organic chrome-free tanning process based on a blend of biodegradable ingredients. The range of subtle cream, blue and beige cuffs have studs riveted into the skins in ethically sourced silk and gold, which are snapped up on both sides of the Atlantic.

These designers are fusing their vision of luxury, recycling and sustainability for a new style of cuff, and yet, technically, jewellery has always encompassed these aspects, either constantly melted down and used again to suit new fashions, or else created with longevity in mind, to be handed down through generations.

The cuff is still a jewel for a generation of independent working women. Armour-like, they maintain a touch of ferocity and the 'don't mess with me' look so appealing to Roman soldiers, but are now fused with a modern sensuality. The cultural history and design of the cuff has been passed along by humans taking journeys, although we now know that travelling also has its negative impacts. New-style cuffs are being made with possible solutions for the future, without damaging the planet, their powerful aesthetics now combined with the positive impact of clearing polluting debris from our environment. Innovative materials have a unique, soft, tactile feel, and although they aren't made from noble metals, they're produced with a different sort of value and meaning, one which, in hindsight, might prove to be lifesaving.

CHAPTER SEVEN

HEAD ORNAMENTS

A headdress is an elaborate or ornamental covering for the head that comes in many forms, from wreaths to hairbands, turbans, tiaras and grandiloquent crowns. Unlike other pieces of jewellery, the head ornament doesn't rest next to the skin; rather, it sits on top of the head, proudly marking the wearer out as an individual and someone who wants to be noticed. Tiaras and diamond diadems are inextricably linked to the aristocracy, so these days, wearing one, no matter what materials it's made from, takes a certain strength of character. Not everyone has the confidence to cycle around London with a coral tiara on their head, as Dame Vivienne Westwood was known to do. The sense of daring, individuality and commitment necessary to wear something so different was exemplified by the late fashion stylist Isabella Blow, who arrived in the office every day wearing elaborate headpieces by English millinery designer Philip Treacy. She wore these wherever she was with a natural composure and eighteenth-century insouciance.

The first objects used for head ornaments were feathers, shells and leaves taken from nature. Later, these motifs were mimicked in metal for headdresses, so it appeared that the wearer had been crowned by nature itself. The head is the first place we look when evaluating someone, and historically, head ornaments have incorporated complex meanings and religious symbolism, telling a story of political power, social status and rank.

The crown is the chief symbol of royal power, and a crowning or coronation is arguably the most significant ritual in which jewellery takes part. We have recently witnessed such a ritual, of course, when the St Edward's Crown, containing some of the oldest gems of Christendom and a regal history stretching back almost a thousand years, was placed on the head of King Charles III. Traditionally, royal crowns were distinguished by their weight and richness of ornamentation, and their placement on the highest point of the monarch's body signified that they must excel all others in virtue. Indeed, their virtues must be as durable as the gold and precious stones used to fashion the crown, whilst its circular shape represents the eternity that will be theirs should the monarch remain virtuous. The mystical and magical properties of the gemstones also aligned with the symbolism of the heavenly crown.

The Latin terms that describe types of crowns – *stemma*, *corona* and *diadema* – were borrowed from the head ornaments of the ancient world. The *stemma*, or wreath, was a garland, the *corona* a small circular coronet and the *diadema* a triangular-shaped piece of cloth worn around the head and tied at the back, all of which indicated rank.

It's entirely possible to imagine why a head 'crowned' with feathers, gold or laurel leaves would imply a royal role, or conjure up a sense of a goddess, god or someone with a divine right. At the very least, by setting themselves apart from others, it demonstrated aspiration and a belief that they were somehow different. Wearing something balanced on your head also requires a specific posture and gait; the chin must be tucked and the back must be kept straight. This lends the postural bearing of a god or goddess or someone special, which can be intensified by the use of dazzling gemstones. You also need to modify your pace, so you can't rush, slump or bend, and slowing down automatically conveys a confident attitude and powerful presence. A person wearing a head ornament inspires awe as they appear to float above everyone else.

WREATHS

Flowers and wreaths were the earliest means of adorning the head. Fashioned in gold, they had the effect of creating a golden halo radiating from the head, highlighting the face and automatically magnifying the wearer's status. These early garlands of flowers, humble leaves of laurel and myrtle and ears of wheat, combined in a horizontal gilded bouquet, projected an image of authority. And they were beautiful, shimmering in the sunlight as the wearer moved. Goldsmiths in ancient Greece crafted some of the most attractive wreath tiaras to adorn the statues of deities and the heads of priests. Often, birds and insects hid amongst the sunlit petals and leaves on trembler springs to aid the illusion of naturalism. A bee sucking pollen or a cicada might be perched on intertwined branches with small olives growing along the twigs. All the components used had a sacred meaning: ears of corn were linked to Demeter, the goddess of the harvest and prosperity; the olive branch associated with Athena; the oak with Zeus; myrtle with Aphrodite, the goddess of practically everything, including healing, the sun and light.

These sacred associations meant wreaths were regarded as symbols of honour. Besides garlands and wreaths associations, the wreaths were regarded as symbols of honour and awarded to victors of musical and athletic contests. They were also an essential part of the dress code for high-status weddings and banquets. The term diadem is also derived from the Greek *diadein*, meaning to bind around, and besides wreaths and garlands there were also gold bands stamped with scrolls, lotus flowers, lilies, honeysuckle, rosettes, figures of deities and Gorgon heads to intimidate enemies.

The Romans adopted the tiara as the supreme indication of rank and honour. Throughout the Roman Empire rich and well-born women and men wore tiaras, flaunting the same flowers and leaves on their golden circlets as the Greeks had done five centuries before. Laurel leaves and berries, sacred to Venus, symbolizing hope over adversity, were mixed with ears of summer corn that seemed to sway in the breeze. The elegance and simplicity of these circlets have been emulated through the centuries, as have certain motifs they used, such as golden ears of wheat, emblematic of fertility and prosperity. A tiara in the Russian Crown Jewels was fashioned from diamonds in the form of bundles of summer corn, cornflowers and buds, making it a favourite to be worn at Romanoff weddings.

During the nineteenth century, jewellers, including Peter Carl Fabergé, who created breathtaking tiaras, sometimes included slender stalks of wheat with a sense of movement and lightness as decorative motifs symbolizing wealth and fertility in the language of flowers and plants. *Épis de blés*, ears of wheat, were a popular design element during the Empire period, linked to the neoclassic aesthetic adopted by Napoleon and his court. When Empress Joséphine commissioned a wheatsheaf tiara made with nine ears of wheat from Marie-Étienne Nitot, the forerunner for Chaumet, to wear for her first official ceremony as sovereign she prompted a resurgence of the motif. By 1811 she'd been outshone by her successor Empress Marie-Louise, who also turned to Nitot to create 150 diamond ears of wheat to decorate her dress and a tiara for her head, which became part of the Crown Jewels. These archival pieces and drawings inspire contemporary wheat sheaves at Chaumet today. Coppery gold wheat ears with ripe brushed grains decorate aigrettes and slender bandeaux designed for modern girls. They are intended to be worn as headbands rather than sovereign status symbols but nonetheless Napoleon would approve. The tiara is inseparable from the image of imperial authority with which he sought to align himself and Roman women were portrayed in paintings wearing golden bandeaux low on their foreheads, so wheat sheaves would have shimmered in the sunlight as they moved, in a similar manner to Chaumet's contemporary versions.

Coco Chanel was born in 1883 during the harvest festival, when the smell of summer wheat filled the countryside air. L'épi de blé, a golden wheat stalk, was a gift from the goddess Ceres to mortals, and Chanel, who grew up to have a superstitious nature, regarded wheat as her personal talisman of good luck and abundance. Her Paris apartment still shimmers with golden incarnations of wheat carvings, lush bouquets and objets d'art, all of which formed part of her history. The emblem remains within Chanel's design *oeuvre* in fine jewels portraying soft ears of corn with fresh emeralds, peridots, aquamarines and diamonds to mimic the grain changing colour as it moves through its lifecycle from young green shoots to yellow ready-to-harvest sapphires. It's a powerful symbol in France, representing the positive energy of a seed that promises it will grow over time. Fields of white-stone wheat are cultivated around the Place Vendôme in homage to archival designs, whilst young jewellers who grew up with strands of wheat placed under their pillows for luck rediscover its fertile history. Using gold, they dip the wheat in a process similar to taxidermy, so the wheat retains the kernel's intricate details and seed ready to open. They make wispy modern headpieces shining with the optimism of summer, reinvigorating an ancient symbol and conveying the full emotion of nature. Wheat endures as a bridal favourite, witnessed by Princess Eugenie, who borrowed a few of Queen Elizabeth's wheat-ear design brooches to pin in her hair for her wedding reception.

THE ORANGE BLOSSOM DIADEM

Flowers and ears of corn adorned the hair of the train bearers to Queen Victoria for her wedding to Prince Albert, and although the fashion at the time was for a tiara to be worn at a marriage, the Queen chose a simple wreath of orange blossom, symbolic of chastity. Marriage was considered the most important occasion in a woman's life, and it was customary for the bride to wear a tiara over her veil, as if at a coronation, a fashion set by Princess Charlotte of Wales, who married Prince Leopold of Saxe-Coburg in 1816 in a dress trimmed with Brussels lace with a blazing wreath of diamond rosebuds and leaves on her head. Thereafter, tiaras were worn as a sign of prestige at European weddings. Possibly, Queen Victoria didn't feel she needed additional diamonds for her head, as she was already wearing what she called her 'Turkish diamond necklace and earrings and Albert's beautiful sapphire brooch'.

Queen Victoria liked to wear tiaras. She was tiny in stature and tiaras gave her a regal presence without the need to wear weighty state crowns. Her favourite was a diamond and sapphire coronet made by jewellers Kitching and Abud, in part because it was designed by her beloved husband Prince Albert, who took a huge interest in her clothes and jewels. The Queen often praised his taste and said, 'he arranged everything for me about my jewels'. The coronet was certainly designed in homage to the central stone, in a shape that echoes the Saxon Rautenkranz, on the shield of the arms of Saxony borne by Prince Albert. The blue stones were used by Albert to be emblematic of their love, with the surrounding diamonds 'crowning' their love. The coronet was one of the most significant jewels of her reign, glittering in the earliest portrait of her by Franz Xaver Winterhalter, which became one of the defining images of her reign throughout the world. It suited Victoria's style, as she liked to exude a youthful and feminine image, wearing her hair in a chignon encircled by a coronet, whilst also being an affirmation of her authority as sovereign.

Prince Albert surprised the Queen one Christmas with a diadem of orange blossoms, in frosted gold and white porcelain, with four green enamel oranges amongst the leaves to represent their children. He had overseen the design personally, and the sprigs of orange blossom and myrtle had been modelled on plants flourishing on the terrace at Osborne House, their home on the Isle of Wight. The flowers had an important significance to the family. When Princess Alexandra of Hesse – Queen Victoria's granddaughter – married Nicholas II of Russia in the Imperial Chapel of the Winter Palace, even though she had the grandeur of the Russian nuptial crown, she still made room for a wreath of orange blossom.

The jewellery owned by Queen Victoria was an expression of national pride and a sign of prosperity for the country, so after the wedding she was always depicted in portraits wearing impressive diamond coronets, tiaras and diadems. After Albert's death, she entered a profound period of grief wearing mourning jewels and vowed she'd never wear coloured gemstones again. The inky-coloured sapphire coronet – 'my beautiful sapphires' as she called them – she deemed suitable for mourning dress and made the exception. She wore the coronet the first time she attended the State Opening of Parliament following

Albert's death, the State Crown relegated to a cushion by her side. It was a small-scale tiara that would have been comfortable for her to wear, but most likely it was the fact that it had been designed by Albert that encouraged her to wear it. They were both sentimentalists, and the coronet would have been a talismanic jewel for her which embodied Albert, whom she would have wanted with her in spirit at Parliament. Wearing the jewel drew attention to her loss, acknowledging her fate with other unhappy widows, whilst not detracting from her role as sovereign. She recognized that any diadem or coronet worn by a royal head was perceived as an unofficial crown.

CAMEOS

Cameos are associated with well-educated tastemakers. Queen Victoria was the cameo afficionado of her age, wearing carved stone portraits, raised in relief, of her children and husband, usually in brooch form. When incised in hardstone, the artistry includes using coloured spots or bands within the stone to emphasize parts of the composition and extraordinary skill to carve complicated scenes of history, battle and mythology in miniature. Throughout history precious gems have always been desirable. However, there have been certain periods of high culture when gems acquired a greater value by being engraved as cameos and mounted in jewellery – during the Hellenistic and Roman periods, the Renaissance as well as the Victorian era. Given that cameos unite the beauty of the gem with the art of the sculptor, I chose to unite them here with the headdress, which is the highest pitch of artistry for the jeweller.

Queen Victoria's cameos were personalized and representative of herself, Prince Albert and their children as the idealized family. Rococo style icon, and mistress of Louis XV, Madame de Pompadour encouraged the art of engraving during the 18th century having a gem carver come to live at Versailles. She bought a drilling machine and was taught to carve scenes and cameos herself in carnelians and topazes. She was painted by the artist François Boucher in *Madame de Pompadour at Her Toilette*, wearing a silver bracelet with a circular cameo of Louis XV's profile. As she would never wear a crown, this cameo expressed her power to the court. Catherine the Great also amassed a collection of cameo pieces, inspired by Byzantine, Greek and Roman design, possibly as a way to further her ties to the Western world, now displayed in the Hermitage Museum. It took Empress Joséphine's impeccable taste of wearing cameos as powerful headdresses, combined with her interest in antiquity, to catapult them into the fashion arena.

A coronation implies regalia and yet by the time Emperor Napoleon took the throne, the royal treasure of the kings of France had been dispersed during the revolution. Despite his lack of royal bloodline, Napoleon wanted to be on the same footing as other European monarchs, and so, like many before him, he used the head ornament as a brilliant device to impress his new position upon the world.

Lacking the dynastic credentials of the Bourbons, Napoleon sought to endorse his reign by the association with ancient Rome. More than anything, it was the glittering tiaras and wreaths at the coronation that transformed the parvenu Bonaparte family into glittering royalty. For his arrival at Notre-Dame on a freezing February day in 1804, Napoleon had dressed himself like a Roman emperor, in a long purple mantle embroidered with bees, a symbol of resurrection, lined with ermine. He led the imperial procession carrying a sceptre and sword, mounted with the 140.64-carat Regent Diamond, with a laurel wreath symbolizing victory encircling his head to align himself with the glories of ancient Rome. Indeed, in the Louvre's painting of the coronation by Jacques-Louis David, Napoleon is depicted with a chiselled profile and head surmounted by laurel leaves redolent of an antique cameo.

Napoleon's coronation crown by Nitot & Fils was made up of a framework of gold arches studded with some of the finest ancient cameos. Beside him sat Joséphine, a shimmery mirage of silver brocade scattered with golden bees and a diadem made of four rows of pearls interlaced with diamond leaves resting on her mass of tiny curls. At the time, Joséphine's jewellery collection was the finest in Europe featuring her large collection of engraved cameos and intaglios. From her first visit to Italy in 1796 as the wife of the conquering hero General Bonaparte, she began acquiring Roman gems, and she was gifted many cameos by family members and generals wishing to court favour. Napoleon wanted to follow in the footsteps of the great Roman emperors, so encouraged both the development of the glyptic arts and the women in his family to follow the cameo fashion. Joséphine requested that her jeweller mount these cameos in attractive settings worthy of their subject matter. She learnt to appreciate virtuoso engraving techniques and to recognize the gods and heroes of mythology and Roman emperors and empresses. No one had ever worn these miniatures as fashionable jewels before, and soon, even patriotic English women at war with France began to emulate the Empress's novel look. As reported by *Le Journal des Dames et des Modes* in 1806, '[a fashionable woman] wears cameos on her belt, cameos on her necklace, a cameo on each of her bracelets, a cameo in her diadem'. Antique carved stones in onyx, sardonyx and jasper or coral, as well as contemporary cameo shells carved in relief, had never been so popular both in France and abroad.

On the Grand Tour, cameos depicting classical subjects were collected along with 'souvenir' bracelets, and travellers visited the studios of gem engravers to have their portrait cut in stone. As impressions were reproduced in plaster, it enabled jewellers to have an unlimited supply of iconography to use in their work, which meant more people could own them.

Signet rings were a popular way to display the art of engraving; Joséphine had Antonio Canova's statue *The Three Graces* reproduced as her seal ring. These small portable sculptures were haunted by vestiges of classical figures, mythological tales of Venus, Cupid, Psyche in the guise of a butterfly, Zeus, Medusa and Hercules and scenes from Greek and Roman history. Cameos communicated cultural interest of an intellectual nature; they were considered 'smart' jewellery. Whilst at her home, Malmaison, nothing gave Joséphine greater pleasure than sitting by a fire and showing her ladies the cameos she was wearing that day, examining every piece. Joséphine's appearance as an empress became an imperative to Napoleon, who took an aggressive interest in the grandeur of his wife's dress and jewels. A shawl that didn't suit his idea of 'majestic' would be thrown in the fire and Joséphine would be demanded to change time and again until he was satisfied. He gave her gifts of diadems, necklaces and precious stones, such as oriental rubies and natural pearls that he brought back from expeditions. In 1811, it's estimated that her jewels had a value of over 5 million francs. Antique gems from the royal treasury were taken out of the Cabinet des Médailles and reset into a parure by court jeweller Nitot & Fils, including a gold leaf tiara featuring Napoleon's favoured cameo portraits of divinities and heroes. Such scenes were a favourite of Napoleon, who aligned himself with the heroism, vanquished enemies, virtue and gallantry of which they spoke to accentuate his right to rule. The cameos were acquired and worn in a cultural atmosphere that demonstrated to the world Napoleon's triumph and the reinstatement of Paris as the centre of luxury and fashion. Cameos suited Napoleon's taste for pomp, splendour and showiness.

Joséphine saw that cameos could take their place with diamonds and pearls as fashionable jewellery. A belief shared by the aristocratic Devonshire family. In 1856, the 6th Duke of Devonshire was to attend Tsar Alexander II's coronation in Moscow. Knowing the family couldn't compete with the dazzling diamond spectacle of the Imperial Romanoff Crown Jewels, he had a spectacular cameo coronet, comb, bandeau and diadem, as part of a seven-piece parure, created for his niece Maria, Countess Granville to wear, lending authority and intellectual grandeur to their presence. The rarity of the Greco-Roman carved gems combined with four gemstones depicting British Tudor monarchs collected by the 2nd Duke of Devonshire were more than a match for Romanoff diamonds and created a talking point which is ongoing today amongst visitors to stately Chatsworth House.

KOKOSHNIKS

Napoleon was descended from minor Italian nobility and used heroic-style cameo head ornaments to elevate himself to 'emperor' status. This was in direct contrast to the Imperial Russian family, who wore the traditional folk kokoshnik headdress. This was worn by country peasants and adopted by the royal family to emphasize a shared cultural history with their fellow countrymen. This was a headdress usually made of fabric, resembling a stiff 'halo', with an undulating outline running across the head. The word *kokoshnik* means cockscomb, and the fabric was fashioned to be as attention-seeking and colourful as possible. Mostly they were made of damask, embroidered and woven with decorative elements representative of the regions where they were made. In the north even peasants embellished the headdresses with river pearls which were plentiful in that area; in the south goose down and woollen embroideries were popular. From its modest beginnings, by the sixteenth century the kokoshnik made it to the Russian court, where it glittered on nearly all Russian ladies' heads, and St Petersburg master jewellers like Peter Carl Fabergé and Bolin were commissioned to create extravagant kokoshnik frames mounted with a profusion of magnificent stones.

The power of the kokoshnik lay in its Russian style and historic Slavic roots. It was instantly recognizable and became a source of strengthening pride both at home and for Russians visiting foreign courts. Worn with unusual ethnic Russian dress, the kokoshnik made a striking and memorable impression, and for this reason it was included as the prescribed tiara shape to be worn in the 1834 edict on court dress issued by Nicholas I. The 'Russian uniform' included a white embroidered silk gown worn beneath a velvet robe with a train and wide hanging 'muscovite' sleeves. Originally the kokoshnik was worn over a veil, giving every woman the appearance of a medieval queen.

Given the complex family ties binding the Romanoffs with other European royal houses, it is not surprising that the kokoshnik was taken up abroad and soon French jewellers like Cartier and Chaumet were producing breathtaking varieties of the style. In London, Garrard made a Russian fringe tiara for Queen Alexandra's twenty-fifth wedding anniversary (her husband was King Edward VII) in 1888. Queen Alexandra was the older sister of Minnie, the Dowager Empress Maria Feodorovna, mother of Tsar Nicholas II, and the two sisters sometimes dressed in the same way to emphasize how alike they looked. The 'Ladies of Society', a group of aristocratic women led by the prime minister's wife, the Marchioness of Salisbury, raised funds to commission a piece of jewellery and asked the Queen directly what she would most like. A 'tiara russe' like the one worn by her sister – a halo-shaped diamond fringe kokoshnik – was her answer. The whereabouts of Minnie's kokoshnik is not known. It is assumed it was taken, dismantled and the stones sold during the revolution. Queen Alexandra's, however, is still frequently worn. It was inherited by Queen Mary and left to Queen Elizabeth II, who wore it consistently throughout her reign; she even lent it to Princess Beatrice for her wedding in 2020.

The Vladimir Tiara had a more dramatic entrance into

the royal collection. The sapphire and diamond headpiece was made by Bolin for the Grand Duchess Vladimir – called the 'grandest of grand duchesses', who was the last Romanoff to escape revolutionary Russia. A British antiques dealer, Albert Stopford, broke into her palace and retrieved the tiara along with some other jewels, smuggling them out of Russia carried in a Gladstone bag. In times of war and financial disruption, jewels have always been a valuable form of convertible wealth, and fortunately the Grand Duchess's family were on hand to assist. The Vladimir Tiara was later bought by Queen Mary, who had a mechanism added so she could change the hanging pendants from pearls to emeralds as took her fancy. The Grand Duchess's sapphire kokoshnik was bought by Queen Marie of Romania, a granddaughter of both Queen Victoria and Tsar Alexander II of Russia.

In spite of the volatility in the years leading up to the 1917 revolution and the myriad signs of unrest and instability, the Russian nobility held onto their extravagant way of life. Cartier sales were booming, with Russian clients providing their largest commissions. Even as late as 1914, the Grand Duchess, with the Countess Orloff-Davidoff, were ordering new tiaras from Chaumet. When Princess Irina, niece of Tsar Nicholas II, married Prince Felix Youssoupoff, she chose a rock crystal tiara from Cartier and the Prince took a pile of his jewels to Chaumet to be remounted for his prospective bride. One emerged as a ruby and diamond tiara, centred on a huge emerald and diamond aigrette set with the Polar Star diamond burning like the setting sun. Only three years later, society and life as they knew it came to an end. The Polar Star diamond headpiece was smuggled out by Youssoupoff but sold to Cartier in 1924 to sustain his family. The remainder of his jewels were found in 1925 in cracks in the walls of the palace from where he'd fled. They were discovered by the communists when altering the palace into the Museum of Military History. The precious cache was declared state property, broken up and sold.

Thus, the role the kokoshnik played in the patriotic portrayal of the splendour of the Imperial court, with all its associated authority and power, was at an end. These jewel-studded, pearl-trimmed kokoshniks, which made blazing masterpieces of the Russian jewellers' art, were an abortive attempt to signify unity between aristocrats and the broad masses of Russian people. Ultimately, however, you could argue that this inflexible style of diadem was representative of feudalism and the Romanoffs' fatal lack of adaptation and modernization, showing just how at odds their extravagant way of life was with that of the average Russian. Their imposing stature, which sparkled at fancy-dress balls and banquets, dwindled during the last days of the Russian empire as the Bolsheviks seized control. The lights went out in the Imperial Hermitage and diamonds were no longer needed to add glitter to kokoshniks for lavish spectacles. The fashion for folk headpieces in Russia was over.

HAIRPINS

Another example of how dramatic political change can affect headdress fashion was the proliferation of diamond aigrettes following the exile of Napoleon. The Emperor had made the tiara into a political symbol, so it wasn't compatible any more with government by republic. As a result, smaller head ornaments were à la mode, and combs, diamond pins and aigrettes became the way French women added sparkle to their hair.

As well as politics, the fashion for tight curls surmounted by a top knot made an impact. This hairstyle required control, so created a need for ornamental combs, decorative stars, suns, crescents, ribbons and bowknot hairpins. Coiffures were embellished with what *Petit Courrier des Dames* described as 'a museum collection of all those invented by art and coquetry over many centuries.'

Inspiration for a new fashion had been found in the Renaissance. The *ferronnière* was a new style of headband encircling the wearer's forehead, usually with a small jewel suspended in the centre, and it was worn for formal evening wear. The idea and name came from Leonardo da Vinci's portrait of *La Belle Ferronnière*, housed in the Louvre Museum, showing a chain across the sitter's brow centred on a coloured stone. The fashion for fifteenth-century beauties was richly decorated hair braids entwined with ropes of white pearls and ribbons pinned with ornamental ruby-headed bodkins atop the head. Young women posed for portraits reflecting the beguiling new look. Piero della Francesca's portrait of Battista Sforza, now in the Uffizi Gallery, shows her wearing a collar of large pearls below her hair, which is plaited with ribbons and arranged with jewelled clusters, and a ruby brooch crowning her head.

The *ferronnière* had another resurgence in popularity during the mid-nineteenth century when hairdresser Marcel Grateau invented a new technique for curling the hair known as the 'Marcel wave'. Women with straight hair now had the opportunity for a head of curls held in place by ravishing ornaments, flowers, hummingbirds and pearls. In some cases, 'transformations' were called for – what we would call extensions or hairpieces – to add the width and volume necessary to grip flirtatious hair accessories in place.

In ancient Egypt, elaborate wigs had been used over shaved heads for reasons of hygiene as well as to enhance feminine beauty, since hair was linked to seduction and eroticism. The curve of the wigs was most often in a striated style of long, parallel, thin streaks, decorated with tassels, braids and in some cases hundreds of golden rings, creating a halo effect. They knew what every subsequent culture realizes – that short hair just doesn't cut it when you want to add embellishments.

Adding hair in the form of wigs and hair pieces, or even backcombing what's there naturally, makes hair ornament-friendly environments. One of the most effective uses of hairpins was captured by Franz Winterhalter when he painted Empress Elisabeth of Austria, who plaited her long hair and secured it with diamond-set stars made by Köchert, the court jeweller, with spectacular effect, almost reaching her lower back.

Complicated hairstyling always requires assistance to maintain the arrangement, so it might as well be ornamental. During the Edo period in Japan, when chignons became large and extravagant, kanzashi hairpins became fashionable. Wood, ivory and tortoiseshell were used with gold, silver and lacquer in naturalistic styles, including trailing vines, using three or four hairpins on each side of the coiffure. These pins would come to reflect the woman's marital status, class and age as much as her personal taste. Later, at the turn of the twentieth century, the art nouveau master jeweller René Lalique took inspiration from Japanese naturalistic design. He understood their fascination with random patterns, mimicking curling iris petals, fallen sycamore seeds and twisting autumnal leaves in diadems and combs using carved horn and tortoiseshell. Like the Japanese, Lalique was a master of atmosphere. In particular, his depiction of the seasons, evoking winter woodlands and sunlight rippling on watery opals in haircombs, paid homage to the role these ornaments played in the ritual of femininity and the poetry of Japanese art and design.

Fazan hairpins and clasps were also part of daily life

in China to keep coiled hair in place, as the dishevelled look was considered impolite. The pins were made with shell, bamboo, horn, jade in copper, silver and gold, often inlaid with beads and kingfisher feathers, in floral patterns or in the form of auspicious animals. Hairpins in the design of a mandarin duck denoted marital happiness; dragons, phoenixes, cranes and the twelve animals of the Chinese zodiac were all lucky creatures. These hair jewels were hung with pendants to frame the face so the petals of peonies and lotus flowers would 'dance' as the wearer moved.

All these embellishments required height and therefore a good head of hair. The ancestral family tiara requires hair setting to be firm and high, so it doesn't move out of place, requiring the support of lashings of hair lacquer. Interestingly, a group of researchers based at the UK's University of Manchester recently examined hair from nine mummies, which, during analysis, revealed a substance made of fatty acids, of animal and plant origins, that coated the hair. There's no proof, but the researchers are convinced this was an ancient Egyptian form of hair gel. Animal fat also produced the eighteenth-century pomade used in Europe to keep hair, which wasn't washed frequently, scented and fresh, plus its stickiness was helpful for styling and attaching hair ornaments. One prodigious style was called the 'pouf', wherein a small cushion was attached to the top of the head to achieve the desired height, with natural or hair pieces curled, frizzed and piled over the cushion, then decorated with all sorts of ornaments, from bows and ribbons to feathers. These styles could be worn for days or weeks at a time.

The fashion for natural-looking hairstyles heralded the demise of hairpins. The *Illustrated London News* complained in 1898 that 'hereditary jewels are even outshone by tiaras of no ancestry whatsoever'. Times were changing, and hair ornaments were no longer mandatory signs of inherited rank nor the sole prerogative of the aristocracy.

During the 1920s, the fashion for bobbed short hair in the West put an end to grand headpieces. New, short, 'boyish' styles such as the 'shingle' couldn't provide a secure home for weighty head ornaments, so their place was taken by the simple outlines of geometric bandeaux, which were worn flat and low on sleek hair.

The final blow to the head ornament took place in 1927, when the first version of liquid shampoo was invented by Hans Schwarzkopf, as it's impossible to anchor a tiara in squeaky-clean hair. A host of head jewels still appear on the runways during the fashion season, looped through hair, adorning foreheads or twinkling from hair partings. Largely, now, tiaras and elaborate hairpins make a striking appearance as sparkly accessories on a bride's special day, when a hairdresser fixes it in place with our modern equivalent of Egyptian hair gel: the trusty aerosol hairspray.

FEATHERS

The term *aigrette* is the French word for egret, and the bird's tufted plumes were used for fashionable head ornaments and hats. *Aigrette* confusingly refers to the long head feathers which adorned Georgian hairstyles as well as the jewel-encrusted head ornament designed to hold them. Often, feather-shaped aigrettes were attached to a diadem, mounted *en tremblant*, with miniature birds, butterflies or hummingbirds buzzing round the pearl- and diamond-set base of the swaying quill. At their peak of popularity these feathers were more costly than an ounce of gold.

If the idea of a headpiece is to draw attention to yourself, a feather gives the wearer an elegant height as well as a delightful air of lightness and fantasy. It is both sumptuous and commanding and, thrust high above the wearer's head, makes a commanding bid to fascinate a room.

When Regency London was the most populous and prosperous city in the world, there was unprecedented social, economic and political change as the industrial revolution beckoned. Stately houses were being constructed as well as new theatres, ballrooms and pleasure gardens for entertainment because leisure time was almost entirely devoted to socializing. As a result, there was a real demand for head jewels, fuelled by the endless social events, including masquerade dances and balls, held every night of the season. Diadems were worn that replicated the grace of feathers in diamond-set mountings in the form of one monumental feather tied with a bow, or two plumes rising to meet each other in the centre of a tiara. These were quite heavy for younger women, for whom aigrettes became all the rage in ostrich, peacock, egret and feathers of birds of paradise. Although Spanish combs and tiaras were considered the more formal hair ornaments for evening wear, many women began to favour the aigrette as a lightweight and less ostentatious jewel. Plus, its height had the flattering effect of lengthening a woman's silhouette, and the gentle movement of the feathers when she nodded her head was coquettish and alluring.

Imagine the dazzling scene at a ball when white jewelled headpieces, pearl chokers, polished steel combs and diamond cornets twinkled everywhere in the candlelight. Stones were foiled at the back to make them even brighter. This was a technique that became popular during the Georgian age, as settings were uniformly closed at the back to give stones a consistent hue. As candlelight meant that soirées and extravagant balls could now be held in the evening, a distinction was made for the first time between 'day' and 'evening' jewellery. During the day emeralds, garnets and rubies brightened with foiling were popular; extravagant diamonds sparkled at night, set off by the candlelight and the silver backing. The American ambassador to the court of George IV described a ball he attended as 'Fairyland. ... no lady was without her plume. The whole was a waving field of feathers. Some were blue like the sky tinged with red, here you saw violet and yellow, there were shades of green. But most were like tufts of snow. The diamonds encircling them caught the light and threw dazzling beams around – it seemed as if a curtain had risen to show a pageant in another sphere.'

Years later, at another royal ball attended by the US ambassador, feathers also dominated. It was 1957 when Jock Whitney was preparing to be appointed ambassador to the Court of St James and he commissioned a tiara for his wife Betsey to wear at Buckingham Palace to be presented to Queen Elizabeth II. He knew they couldn't compete with the ancestral tiaras that would be on show that night, so instead he wanted to emphasize Betsey's American roots – and therefore her republican background. With this in mind, Fulco di Verdura created the American Indian tiara. Bristling with feathers wrought with diamonds and gold, which were bunched into groups curling upwards from a gold band, the headdress perfectly expressed her homeland using symbolism rooted in the New World.

There was a sense of poignancy and melancholy that an old world had come to an end following the 1971 costume ball thrown by Baron and Baroness Guy de Rothschild. The Proust Ball was an extravagant spectacle to celebrate the centenary of the writer's birth and was held at the luxurious Rothschild Château de Ferrières outside Paris. The guest list embodied beauty, aristocracy, power, talent and fortune – as well as royalty in the guise of Princess Grace of Monaco. Sir Cecil Beaton took the photographs amongst banks of mauve and violet branches of orchids, the vast winter garden was transformed into a ballroom and crystal chandeliers shimmered in every window of the castle, lit outside by blazing torches. Guests made their way up the theatrical grand double staircase serenaded by a Gypsy band, led through dark corridors by carmine-clad footmen holding candelabras into the Tapestry Room for a lavish dinner. The grandiosity of the event was illustrated by Lady Lambton, who wore two tiaras: one on her head and another around her neck.

Feathers were out in force on the heads of famous guests adhering to the costume dress code, whilst vying to outdo each other in splendour. The glamorous Baroness, who was wearing ivory silk Saint Laurent, flaunted white feathers in her hair, matching a fan of ostrich feathers garlanded with pearls, whilst the Duchess of Windsor's feather was so large in size that, Beaton reported, it slapped the face of her host every time she turned her head. Actress Marisa Berenson looked ravishing dressed as the Marchesa Casati wearing a black wig of curls loaded with aigrettes with black jet necklaces. Arguably, however, it was Elizabeth Taylor's black egret feathers that drew the most attention and which were remembered above all.

Wearing a statement headpiece was not unfamiliar to Taylor, having donned a tiara at the 1957 Academy

Awards and the Cannes Film Festival. At the ball she was dressed as the actress Ida Rubinstein, wearing black taffeta and lace, with a Van Cleef & Arpels fringe necklace woven into her hairline to hold the sensational feathers in place, which fluttered over her raven hair like a pennant, drawing the gaze of 350 people to the diamond on her neck. Hanging on a black ribbon was the most famous diamond in the world at the time: the 68-carat Taylor-Burton Diamond.

Taylor sparkled at the centre of an evening which marked the end of an era. These were the last people to witness a festivity on such a grand scale; it was the last of the twentieth century's legendary parties. New winds of change were blowing, and the days of such conspicuously profligate balls were over. A few years later, Guy de Rothschild handed the Ferrières castle over to the University of Paris. Like the expiration of the kokoshnik during the final days of the Russian Empire, the Proust Ball proved to be the last hurrah for the aigrette.

Our interest in feathers endures, however, and is still a popular jewellery motif, set in stony motion hanging from pendants and earrings. In the world of fashion, where anything can be a headdress, feathered aigrettes using gilt, fabric roses and crystals make show-stopping pieces in the pages of fashion magazines, bringing an otherworldliness to the human form. An exuberance of snowy plumes on a model never fails to make an exotic, scene-stealing picture of heady luxuriance. Instead of costume balls, young girls today now mostly use feathers as alluring summer circlets at music festivals to get themselves noticed à la Taylor, like downy flags of individualism amongst the swaying crowds.

WARBONNETS

Although the high-flown jewelled aigrette is no longer worn, the phrase 'feather in one's cap' endures in many cultures. Usually it denotes achievement of some kind, whether in education or a specific skill, and yet its origins are of a more bloodthirsty nature. From the Native Americans to the Masai, tribal people would use the most extravagant plumes of the birds they hunted to decorate themselves, to show off a hunter's prowess. In the Highlands of Scotland, the custom of sticking a quill in a cap from the first gamebird killed persists, albeit now more as a fashion statement for country-style hats. The late Queen Elizabeth II added feathers to her hats on walks around Sandringham in Norfolk. Three white plumes of the ostrich *Struthio camelus* have featured on the heraldic badge of the Prince of Wales since the fourteenth century, when they were adopted by Edward, the Black Prince, following his victory at the Battle of Crécy.

There are a number of bloodthirsty references relating feathers to the killing of enemy combatants. The English writer and traveller Richard Hansard wrote in 1599 on a trip to Hungary, 'It hath been an antient custom among them [Hungarians] that none should wear a fether but he who killed a Turk, to whom onlie yt was lawful to shew the number of his slaine enemys by the number of fethers in his cappe'.

Feathers in caps became about skill, determination and courage. Lord Horatio Nelson, admiral of the Royal Naval fleet which defeated the French in the Battle of the Nile in 1798, received a jewelled feather in his cap in honour of his leadership. The Sultan of the Ottoman Empire, Selim III, presented Nelson with the 18cm-long, 300-diamond-set Plume of Victory taken from his turban in gratitude for the victory. The central diamond, the Ottoman star, was powered by clockwork to rotate and sparkle in candlelight. Nelson, as the first non-Muslim to receive a *chelengk*, feathered his felt bicorn hat with the dazzling military decoration. He asked permission from the King to wear it as part of his official uniform and fashioned it like a turban jewel for the remainder of his life, sparking a craze for similar jewels in England.

There's a long Native American tradition of adding a feather to the headdress of any warrior who performs a brave act, which led to impressive shows of plumage of indigenous birds. Feathers are a significant part of self-adornment, emblematic of status, defiance and bravery. It's thought the Sioux were the first tribe to adopt the custom for ceremonial purposes, as well as for protection against the elements and to confer status.

Each feather was planted into a warbonnet, a feathered

headdress traditionally worn by leaders of the American Plains Indian Nations who've earned a place of respect in the tribe due to an act of courage or to commemorate an achievement. Sometimes, the first feather was gained upon becoming an adult member of the tribe, but even then, the recipient would spend days meditating in preparation to receive it. When enough feathers had been won, a head-dress would be made and intricately woven with animal skins, like deer and ermine, embellished with tribal-designed beadwork. White eagle feathers with brown tips from younger eagles represented strength, whilst the brown feathers from older eagles stood for wisdom. The most prized feather to receive was that of the golden eagle, believed to be a messenger of God, and this was only earned through hardships, strength and loyalty. The more feathers a bonnet contained, the more accomplished the wearer. Native American women wore headbands of woven deer hide strips with beads, wampum or quillwork, with a single feather from an eagle, egret, hawk or crane inserted at the back of the head.

These feathered emblems also provided spiritual pro-tection, as the fur and feathers of sacred animals used were believed to endow the wearer with their power. Warrior chiefs wearing golden eagle feathers, connected to a buckskin beaded crown with fur and red-tailed hawk and kestrel feathers hanging from either side, was like Napoleon wearing a laurel leaf crown to reinforce his sanctity and legitimize his right to rule.

There are 565 federally recognized tribes in the US alone, and the type of headdress worn by each one depends on their customs and the available materials. There is insult when individual tribes' practices are lumped together by fashion or film to represent the whole in a theatrical manner and also when these customs and dress are appropriated by non-Native Americans. During the 1990s, a feathery *Vogue* story caused offence when the late Corinne Day photographed the model Kate Moss wearing a headdress. A Chanel tribute to the beauty of craftsmanship showing Native American headdresses in a 2013 runway show also received mixed reviews.

Nowadays, Native elders fear for the demise of the warbonnet and the erosion of the First Nations' cultural values, as younger people don't have the spiritual knowledge to create the headdresses. They foresee a time when traditional headdresses no longer play a part in pow-wows and ceremonies. Small wonder there is sensitivity as they passionately try to hold onto their heritage and culture.

Turbans

As well as the warbonnets of Native American tribes, there are other examples to be found of cultures where the practice of wearing feathered head ornaments has also largely vanished.

The Maharaja of Patiala had a magnificent turban

ornament in the form of a large diamond feather at least 10 inches long, edged by a fringe of pear-shaped emeralds, each one almost priceless. At one time, some of the most beautiful jewels were fashioned as sarpeches, ornaments to be displayed on the front of a nobleman's turban. The headdress dates from 230 BCE Mesopotamia and has a symbolic significance to many different religions and cultures. For many, the turban is a way of identifying themselves with a group or culture, and it signifies respect, honour and dedication to a certain way of life. Turbans and gems and jewels have been an integral part of daily wear across classes and faiths.

In both Asia and Europe, the word 'maharaja' means 'great king' and conjures up a vision of a ruler in a bejewelled turban, whose authority was absolute and who had wealth beyond measure. For the purposes of this book, I'm using the term maharaja for ruler, although there was a wide range of titles across the subcontinent, such as nizam, nawab, raja, rao and others. Turban jewels were originally a royal emblem and remain one of the rich cultural objects of kingship that define their era. The ornaments were a sign of rank and wealth, as they were designed as jewelled brooches dazzling with huge gemstones and often backed by plumes of feathers to confer greater panache to the wearer. In the book *Maharaja*, Joanne Punzo Waghorne explains that it was a fundamental duty of a maharaja to appear to his people *samalamkara*, meaning fully ornamented and enabled, to ensure in some way the health and well-being of his subjects. 'In this context the lavish ornamentation of the maharajas of India becomes religious necessity', she writes, 'not a frivolous extravaganza.' Many appeared weighted – on their head, neck, chest, arms, fingers and ankles – with ravishing bright precious stones and pearls.

Although the princes expressed their authority without crowns, the royal device was clearly absent from the coats of arms distributed to the princes in 1877, following the Royal Titles Bill, when Queen Victoria was proclaimed Empress of India. Henceforth, any prince adopting a crown would seem disloyal, so instead, turban ornaments became increasingly regal and elaborate, even spreading horizontally in the manner of a European tiara, complemented by ropes of gemstone beads encircling the turban. The Queen began a love affair with the exotic and faraway country of India, adding the Durbar Room to her Isle of Wight home Osborne House, created by architect Bhai Ram Singh, which boasted impressive Indian plaster work. The Queen's obsession with India was rivalled only by the Indian princes' love affair with the French jewellery houses.

The fantastically decorated princes became a frequent sight in Europe following the First World War, where they travelled to explore modernism in art and culture and return with new ideas encompassing everything from progressive leadership to infrastructure networks and educational and social reform. Le beau monde was enthralled by the undreamed-of exoticism, grandeur and

261

sheer size of the gems that accompanied them. One can just imagine the scene when a maharaja arrived in Paris, sometimes accompanied by an entourage of forty servants wearing pink turbans, along with twenty dancing girls and guards carrying metal chests filled to the brim with a treasury of emeralds, diamonds, pearls and rubies. Flashing from a turban would be a robin's egg-sized emerald with flowerhead design, surrounded by large table-cut diamonds draped with pearls and spinels. Every French jeweller took inspirational note of the Indian style to intrigue their European clients with new pieces. An artistic exchange grew and gathered momentum as the maharajas became celebrated patrons of French jewellers, bringing loose precious stones to be mounted into European-style modern pieces by Boucheron, Cartier and Chaumet. The jewel *maisons* in turn began fashioning jewels for European nobility using Indian colours and design. Influential women such as Daisy Fellowes and Mrs Cole Porter subsequently wore the new Cartier leaf-carved ruby, emerald and sapphire 'Hindu'-inspired jewels which became known as 'Tutti Frutti'.

By now, lightweight platinum had been introduced into European jewellery, enabling expansive and delicate settings for diamond sarpeches and aigrettes commissioned from the great houses of Paris and London. These pieces merged the technological innovation of the West with Indian design and contributed to maharajas combining their ancient role of kingship with a modern princely identity. Jagatjit Singh, the Maharaja of Kapurthala, had a turban ornament designed at Cartier in 1927 for his Golden Jubilee with a central hexagonal emerald weighing 177.40 carats. Immediately, he had his portrait painted wearing the impressive turban ornament by society artist Marcel Baschet.

Kapurthala's dazzling Western-style jewels inspired Sir Bhupinder Singh, the Maharaja of Patiala, to follow suit. When he travelled to Paris, his retinue settled into thirty-five suites at the Ritz Hotel before he crossed the Place Vendôme to make one of the largest special jewellery orders in the history of the square. He asked Louis Boucheron, son of founder Frédéric, to set 2,000 carats of white, blue and yellow diamonds, rare grey pearls and 14,000 emeralds, which were delivered wrapped in coloured diaphanous fabric, into modern interpretations of Indian jewels. The pieces blended traditional Indian ceremonial ornament with the prevailing fashion for art deco styles, and the commission was so large they invited Cartier to help them complete it, not knowing Cartier had also been working on major re-settings of his jewellery since 1925. Such was the number of the Maharaja's spare gemstones, the resulting 149 pieces included belts, collars, turban ornaments, aigrettes, armbands and sautoirs. Today, inspired by the order, Boucheron create modern sarpech-like delicate diamond hair brooches, the paisley shape and wispy lines reminiscent of a peacock feather, echoing a grand aigrette from the past.

India's cultural impact endures to this day in French and British jewellery design, and turban ornaments demonstrate the fact that neither the crowns nor monarchs of whatever race would yield power in India. The jewels were a modern manifestation of the traditional role of the maharaja as a patron of the arts and possessor of the rare and wonderful, and show how they were borrowing, adapting and transforming from the outside world to create something uniquely Indian, whilst opening the Western jewellers' minds to a whole new world of artistic possibilities. Many of these treasures have since been lost or reset, so when one does surface at auction, it provokes passionate bidding. A mid-eighteenth-century Mughal turban ornament of diamonds, emeralds and enamel was sold at Christie's auction house in Geneva in 2012 for a record 4.45 million francs, proving that when power is embodied in beautiful objects, their potency is never really extinguished.

CORONATION CROWNS

Ceremonies may change and modernize over the centuries, but not our devices of ritual, of which the crown is the centrepiece.

The visceral power of the St Edward's Crown, which currently sits atop the head of King Charles III, lies in its historical significance, which encompasses almost 1,000 years of monarchy. Named after St Edward the Confessor, the last English Anglo-Saxon king who was canonized by Pope Alexander III, versions of the crown have been used to crown English and British monarchs since the thirteenth century. On one occasion, it was also used to crown a Queen Consort. Following his scandalous divorce from his first wife Catherine of Aragon, Henry VIII was keen that Anne Boleyn be viewed as the legitimate queen. She was already pregnant, so the St Edward's Crown would acknowledge her role as Queen and mother to what he must have believed was his long-awaited son and heir.

At the close of the English Civil War in 1649 when King Charles I was executed, gold was melted down and turned into coins and jewels sold from the Royal Collection by Parliament to fund the new government. When the British republican experiment failed and Charles II was invited to return and take the throne, he wanted to restore the prestige of the monarchy with displays of splendour. A coronation would project an air of majesty, pomp and ceremony. With this in mind, he set about recovering as much as possible from the Commonwealth dispersals and from nobles who'd acquired royal gems and were now eager to court favour from the new King by returning them. He commissioned new regalia and a crown, using vestigial materials from the original as well as some of the saved historic gemstones.

Goldsmith Robert Vyner created what we know today as the St Edward's Crown, from the medieval design, with crosses pattée, fleurs-de-lis and arches set with a colourful array of precious rubies, amethysts, topazes, sapphires, garnets, peridots and tourmalines. The mystical properties of the stones in a way celebrate each new reign brightly glinting with hope and faith. It has a red velvet cap and ermine band but, created from solid gold, it weighs nearly 5 pounds. The desired result was successful, as diarist Samuel Pepys confirmed when describing the splendours of the coronation, concluding that 'I may now shut my eyes against any other objects, or for the future trouble myself to see things of state and shewe, as being sure never to see the like again in this world'.

The St Edward's Crown has been used at the coronation of each successive sovereign of the British throne ever since, at the sacred moment of crowning, and only three people are entrusted to touch it: the Crown jeweller, the Archbishop of Canterbury and the monarch.

The most historic royal gem is the St Edward's sapphire, which confusingly rests atop of the Imperial State Crown, not the St Edward's Crown, which the monarch wears throughout their reign following the coronation. It is not a large gem. No one seems to know the exact carat weight, and there are far larger and brighter stones in the Crown Jewels. And yet this rose-cut stone looms large in British history. In 1066 the sapphire was buried with King Edward the Confessor, in front of the High Altar in Westminster Abbey, but his coffin was subsequently moved several times and at one point, opened. At some stage, the ring on his finger was removed and for 300 years put on show in Westminster Abbey, where visitors came to view it as a holy relic and saintly object.

When Henry VIII made himself head of the Church of England, he removed the sapphire and took it for himself and had it mounted together with the ruby from Thomas Becket's tomb in Canterbury Cathedral. After Henry's death, Edward's sapphire was removed from the ring and Queen Elizabeth I wore it like a diadem on her forehead. Following the execution of King Charles I in 1649, however, the stone vanished, most likely smuggled out of the country during the Civil War. It surfaced during the reign of King George III and was bought on behalf of his son, the Prince Regent, by the English banker Thomas Coutts for the princely sum of £4,000 and was returned to England and the crown where it remains as a witness to royal history. As does the bright green peridot stone in the St Edward's Crown, reflecting its prescient symbolism of renewal and hope for each new monarch. It is a contradictory crown that embodies the past whilst representing the future.

At one time, the Imperial family of Russia had the most impressive jewel collection in Europe. The Great Imperial Crown was first used in the coronation of Catherine the Great and lastly to crown Tsar Nicholas II. It was made in 1762 by the court jeweller Georg Friedrich Ekart and stone setter Jérémie Pauzié, who were inspired by the Byzantine Empire to fashion the crown in the style of a mitre with two half spheres divided by a floral garland to represent the joining of the Eastern and Western empires. As Pauzié wrote in his memoir, he had been asked by Empress Catherine to check the treasury and break everything that wasn't in modern taste. He took all the biggest stones to make what he described as 'one of the richest objects ever existed in Europe'. Consequently, it is adorned with 4,936 diamonds running in patterns across the surface, with the two hemispheres bordered by rows of pearls, from which a central arch rises to hold a 398.72-carat spinel. Everything was designed to project the power of the Tsar. The size and quality of the gemstones were stupendous, whilst royal fleur-de-lis motifs were used with diamond oak leaves representing power and strength, with a cross above to signpost the Christian faith of the sovereign, the divine right of the monarchy. The crown was emblematic of all Imperial authority – until it wasn't.

Overnight, after the October Revolution in 1917, the imperial regalia was taken for safekeeping at the Kremlin armoury before being stored in a secure place by representatives of the people. From the opulent Winter Palace, the crown landed on a tabletop under the watchful gaze of members of the government committee, and the odd journalist taking a look, who played with the idea of being a tsar, trying the crown on for size. Discussions were had about a possible sale with French and British experts, but the advice received was that it would be unlikely to attract its historic worth. The actual materials – the diamonds and gems – had a straightforward price, but what value could ever be placed upon its unique and extraordinary stately history, not to mention its bloody conclusion? Technically it still remains a crown even when there is no ceremony, ritual or service in which it plays the starring role. In the Kremlin showcase today, it is a fantastically pretty work of art that attracts visitors as a glittering historical leftover from an ancient regime.

Nearly 300 carats of diamonds from Catherine the Great's wardrobe decorate the arches of the Russian Nuptial Crown, which was worn by all the grand duchesses and wives of grand dukes on their wedding day with a diamond tiara. The crown was bought at auction in 1927 by American businesswoman and cereal heiress Marjorie Merriweather Post, who would show it off to guests at her Hillwood Estate, serving up to 600 people at her dining room table using Russian porcelain. Viewing the exquisite crown of Russia's powerful erstwhile rulers must have surely mesmerized her guests, no matter their political persuasion.

Another magnificent treasure that sits in a cabinet rather than atop a monarch's head is the Pahlavi Crown, which was last used in 1967 at the coronation of the Shah of Iran. It glistens with an astonishing 3,380 diamonds and a 60-carat yellow diamond centred in a starburst of white gems, trimmed with natural pearls and emeralds. It's also an example of precious stone layering in depth. A white aigrette flutters from the crown's apex, making a noble statement now from the Treasury of National Jewels in Tehran.

History relates that crowns don't always rest easy on royal heads. Traditionally, the day after a revolution, the primary concern is to secure the crown for the people or to destroy it altogether as the embodiment of everything they seek to overthrow. As we have seen, this was the case in Britain during the Civil War, when Parliament had the St Edward's Crown melted down, since it was regarded by republican Oliver Cromwell as symbolic of the 'detestable role of kings'. In 1887, prior to the sale of the French Crown Jewels, a deputy of the Third Republic stated, 'A democracy that is sure of itself and confident in the future has a duty to rid itself of these objects of luxury, devoid of usefulness and moral worth'. Exquisite tiaras, crowns and diamond jewels worn by kings and queens were auctioned. It was claimed they were frivolous, and yet this only underlined their power. These were the symbols of monarchy, so they had to be sold or broken up to prevent a restoration of the throne. Without a crown, they reasoned, there could not be another king, because the crown represents the bloodline of the sovereign.

The American jeweller Tiffany & Co. snapped up more than half of the treasures sold in red leather boxes marked 'Diamants de la Couronne'. Some years later, to great excitement, Mrs Arthur Paget arrived at the Devonshire Costume Ball – the dress code of which was stipulated as 'allegorical or historical costume before 1815' – dressed as Cleopatra, in a costume made by Worth, wearing the French Crown Jewels she'd purchased from Tiffany. And yet, she'd had them remodelled. Detached from their original design and historical context, she was, in essence, simply wearing an arrangement of beautiful and valuable gemstones.

Jewels have more lives than cats. Other people's glittering historic hand-me-downs are often available to the highest bidder. Kim Kardashian purchased an amethyst and diamond cross worn by Princess Diana from Christie's recently, whilst Marjorie Merriweather Post must have been a sucker for a doomed royal story, as she snapped up Queen Marie Antoinette's diamond earrings as well as a tiara once owned by Empress Marie Louise.

Every jewel is linked to memory and evokes the past, but head ornaments are often the most visual sign of an era when we thought, lived and behaved differently. Whilst other monarchies retain a crown now purely as a national symbol, the extraordinary spectacle of the St Edward's Crown still glows in the present with a purpose, whilst mirroring an ancient past. Britain is the only European monarchy still using its regalia for the consecration ceremony of crowning the sovereign, and I for one hope it remains a living part of our island's story and isn't relegated to the status of museum showpiece.

Jewellery is very forgiving and moves with the times – shifts in social attitudes, fashion changes or variations between generations often lead to reworkings. That's part of its silent magic. Modern life, however, has sent the head ornament into retreat. Precious head ornaments are now rarely seen and even royals wear them less frequently. Largely now they are worn at weddings, where the bride still dresses as if being crowned and fancies being queen for a day at least, or at the odd state banquet. One notable exception, of course, are costume balls, like Sir Elton John's charity event, with a dress code of white tie and tiaras. There you might see the Countess of Derby wearing the historic Derby Tiara alongside model Naomi Campbell dressed like a Renaissance princess in loaned head sparkles.

Whether crafted from fake rhinestones, crystals or feathers, head ornaments will never completely disappear, because it's part of our human nature to set ourselves apart. All it takes is some ironic self-confidence and chutzpah to carry it off and a little poise to keep it in place.

CONCLUSION

And what of the future? Above all, the jewel displays an art form, the hands of other human beings who've created it reside there in the skills of the goldsmith transforming a sheet of metal into something delicate, light, pierced and wearable, which is a kind of magical alchemy. That's a practice and an enriching shared history wherever we are from that links us around the world. Each jewelled object's biography is a collision of cultures and influences – a mini-course in world history from human beings who've travelled and pooled ideas and experiences. The cult of the beautiful and sense of wonder that a jewel provokes can be unifying.

Certainly, I hope that new designers will come and challenge our ideas of what a jewel should look like. I like to imagine the practice of tattooing and jewels might combine in some way and we can pepper our skin directly with jewels. Our relationship with technology will certainly be expressed in the future of jewel-making. We are already recycling elements of old smartphones and when dug up in years to come, pieces will speak of the time in which we live and our modern idolization of technology. Artificial intelligence is already creating a paradigm shift in how jewellery is created and sold, with software platforms outsourcing CAD (computer aided design) and 3D metal printing manufacturing. Jewellery makers now have the technology to enable them to make pieces on a greater scale than ever before.

We can all now try pieces on digitally online, and AI with 3D hologram technology means we can study stones and jewels in real time on our phones and even contribute to the design process. Machine learning can be used in jewellery design in conjunction with hand crafting. AI is transforming countless industries and jewellery design won't be the exception. For example, the use of data-driven design in the manual process or an algorithm-driven process to create a design automatically. It could take over more time-consuming tasks at the start of the design process and increase efficiency whilst allowing designers more time to be productive in other areas. The centuries-old method of jewellery-making being a magical amalgam of sketch, material and craftsmanship always includes something of the era in which it was created. Jewellery is never developed in isolation but expresses societal change.

So, jewellery will reflect current changes like AI and the crypto market. Case in point: Tiffany & Co. recently targeted the CryptoPunks community – holders of a style of pixelated avatar sold as an NFT – offering them the chance to transform their avatar into a custom necklace, which would be produced as an NFT and a real-world gold, diamond and gemstone necklace. CryptoPunks had to purchase an NFTiff pass, which Tiffany & Co. created in collaboration with blockchain creator Chain, to access the necklace paid for in Ethereum. The real world inspired the NFTiff, which was, in turn, inspired by the metaverse.

Technology is positively influencing modern jewellery collections in terms of inspiration, materials and transparency. Distinguished fine jeweller Hemmerle uses antique cameos as *objets trouvés* whereas young brand Oushaba salvages parts of discarded mobile phones so electrical components considered waste take centre stage in their jewellery. The age-old motifs of hearts, triangles and snakes at Prada are all produced with pure gold recycled from electronic parts, such as smartphone circuits. Each piece comes with an electronic card which, when tapped by your phone, can reveal details from supplier to certification for responsibly sourced gold. Likewise, actress and writer Michaela Coel stepped out on the red carpet recently wearing gold earrings made with Single Mine Origin gold which had their own QR code. With the code you can witness the journey of the gold in the mine, meet the miners and community and the environmental projects surrounding it. It's total traceability and transparency.

New pieces might be embedded with an NFT tag, which when read by a smartphone could trigger memories and digital memorabilia of the family and special moments. Can jewellery NFTs make a real connection in the virtual world? Time will tell. Crypto enthusiasts promise the NFT will last forever, but physical jewellery already does that. In addition, there's the portable wealth aspect of jewels and stones. In a volatile world we need the real thing. There have been many times in history when fleeing with your jewellery to sell might be all that stands between you and starvation. Maybe the benefit is to make a piece hyper-personalized, like a jewelled time capsule of your life. In effect, algorithms will allow machines to become co-creators of a piece of jewellery. Our understanding of what's precious will be redefined and challenged, and the recycling of plastic included with gold will be mixed by metallurgists to create new materials. Jewellery is also beginning to contain modern wearable technology, such as smartwatches and fitness trackers, and now wedding tech rings can allow you to monitor the heartbeat of your loved one. But we won't lose the human element in creation as we need eyes to notice the changing world and how people are living, as well as the hands to implement a new idea in jewellery.

I don't see space as the final frontier to change jewellery; there have been sparkly constellations of stars, planets and the night skies emulated in jewellery forever. Technology will provide the revolution. Jewellery is about how you communicate, and in the future it's this idea of connectivity that is changing. Currently, how we want to dress when we see ourselves in a digital form seems to be quite traditional, as brands introduce us slowly to jewelled NFTs to wear both in the metaverse and, in some cases, in the real world too. Jewels are like signals that help us to understand each other, and I can't see that changing. Indeed, maybe we will need to rely on it more as we enter these strange new virtual territories. The notion of jewellery as a way to bond, as well as an emotional treasure with an inbuilt sense of preciousness for the individual, is just as relevant for online gamers as it was for early humans.

How sci-fi will jewellery be in the future? ChatGPT launched relatively recently and is progressing fast, but is in its infancy as to how far it can go. There's a chorus of voices urging that we think about this technology which has the capacity to make decisions for us, cautioning about the possible scenarios in which it will have far more knowledge than we do. Digital intelligence is different to human intelligence and will communicate in ways that humans can't. Would it step in to change our rituals? That's a question that no one can answer right now, and yet I would argue that jewellery in this scenario becomes even more crucial, to remind the world that you are a human with thoughts and feelings.

The modern world is difficult to navigate, and I hope there will be a surge of protest jewellery as young people assert their opinions and define a new role for themselves. Jewellery can be a powerful tool for humanity to acknowledge feelings of identity and isolation and an emblem to draw attention to changes they need. As the natural world is threatened, I see young artists wanting to represent it in their work, and jewellery can be sustaining in a way for groups to get attention. We've witnessed that before; in jewellery design, the past and present collide to craft something new for the future. These small objects aren't merely symbolic passive decorations – they mean things which can motivate people and make things happen, and as such become active participants in the formation of identity and change.

At the end of the day, it's the durability of jewels and stones that can survive and our wish for immortality is where the human psyche always returns. Deep in our consciousness we recognize jewels as the essence of memento mori, which encourage us to honour those people who have gone by living our lives to the fullest. Whether we stare into the blackness of the night sky or dark mysteries of the metaverse, there is a nothingness in eternal space. Jewellery provides a type of comfort against the unknown and our questions that can't be answered, which was probably the same motivation for early man drilling shells to wear as he looked out of the world beyond the Blombos Cave.

Jewels are links to each other through history, proving we are not alone. The eternal challenge of the human condition – how to live, love and die – are expressed in jewellery. Whilst we remain social creatures, jewellery will always provide something for us to hold onto. This book is an acknowledgement of that need.

ACKNOWLEDGEMENTS

I am indebted to my editor, Alison Macdonald, who listened to my podcast and liked it enough to commission this book and help me realise it through to publication. I owe a huge thanks to Natasha Cowan and Tim Thornton, the producer and editor respectively of my podcast, for supporting me from the very beginning when I first approached them with my modest ambition to start a podcast during the Covid-19 pandemic.

I'm grateful to Laurie Robertson and Samantha Brace at Peters Fraser and Dunlop for their wise counsel. To my cohorts in the jewellery industry – too many to mention – who allow me the benefit of their wisdom, knowledge, patience and, in many cases, precious friendship. My friends and family who are always generous with their suggestions, contributions and support, especially when tolerating my absence when I'm obsessively chasing down the next jewelled nugget.

Of course, I owe so much to the guests on my podcast who have generously shared their sparkling stories and expertise with me. I'm delighted to add voices from so many different spheres and professions and I'm grateful to each and every one of them.